YOU CAN TALK TO ANYONE

EASILY ENGAGE IN CONVERSATION USING PROVEN COMMUNICATION SKILLS AND FORGE STRONG INTERPERSONAL CONNECTION

ELLEN DAWSON

Copyright © 2023

All rights reserved

All rights to this book are reserved. No permission is given for any part of this book to be reproduced, transmitted in any form or means, electronic or mechanical, stored in a retrieval system, photocopied, recorded, scanned, or otherwise. Any of these actions require the proper written permission of the publisher.

DISCLAIMER

Disclaimer all knowledge contained in this book is given for informational and educational purposes only. The author is not in any way accountable for any results or outcomes that emanate from using this material. Constructive attempts have been made to provide information that is both accurate and effective, but the author is not bound for the accuracy or use/misuse of this information.

CONTENTS

Introduction   9

1. A Current Feeling of Disconnection   17
2. Positive Health Benefits of Being With Others   41
3. Proven Conversation Techniques to Help You Connect   69
4. Engage in Live Social Connections   103
5. How to Find or Create a Conversational Group   127
6. Leave Isolation Behind With Great Friendships   149

Conclusion   171
References   177

I want to express my thanks to my daughter, Kerry Thurlow. Without her help, this book would not have been possible.

INTRODUCTION

It doesn't matter why you feel isolated, whether it's health issues, trauma from the global pandemic, the loss of a loved one, job loss, or the ongoing upheaval in the world. You're here now, and you can help yourself.

Building deep and meaningful friendships and strong interpersonal relationships has always been challenging for many, myself included.

Today, social stability is changing, and many say that the change isn't for the better. In 2020, we experienced a prolonged lockdown and extended social isolation caused by COVID-19. Alone in our homes, we watched helplessly as medical professionals became heroes as they fought an invisible virus that mercilessly snatched the lives of countless people, some of them our own loved ones. That virus is still present in our lives today.

When the lockdown ended, we tried to pick up where we left off, but our world changed while we were away. In the United States, politics became more divisive and polarizing. Deficiencies in our healthcare system were glaring. Women were leaving the workforce due to the lack of affordable childcare. In the wider world, current events like the war between Ukraine and Russia, political unrest in the Middle East, and the emergence of new strains of COVID in China can be unsettling and deepen feelings of isolation.

In the middle of our unpredictable and uncertain world, some people are surprisingly calm and unbothered by how the world keeps transforming. Many of us are not okay! Like me, these events may have transformed you into an entirely different person. As a result, I questioned many things, including my relationships with friends and family. The more I doubted myself, the more I became overwhelmed with insecurity and social anxiety.

My internal chaos intensified my feelings of emotional isolation and kept me socially isolated. Even in the company of others, I could not shake off feelings of isolation. Of course, I didn't like this socially isolated version of myself, but it was hard work to break out of my shell and be the carefree, social person I once was.

As much as I would like to label myself a psychic or an expert in psychology, I am neither. But, I have firsthand experience of social isolation and loneliness in a world where everyone else seems to have their lives together.

I have always been quiet and shy since my childhood in rural Connecticut. It didn't help that my family was large and boisterous. Because of my personality, I was constantly getting lost in the crowd. People don't tend to notice the quiet, shy one. As I grew up, I realized I needed to learn to speak up and stand up for myself. Of course, the process took work and a long time, but I eventually mastered being more outgoing. I learned to talk comfortably with people, whether they were familiar or not. As an adult, this formerly shy person became comfortable creating, organizing, and hosting face-to-face conversational groups rather than just participating in conversations.

Before the pandemic, I was living my best life, going about my daily routine, participating in exercise classes, attending church, and hosting groups of family and friends. One of my favorite activities is taking part in various conversational groups. A conversational group is any group of people who meet regularly for a conversation focused on one or more areas of life. I have a small group of friends that meets at a local coffee shop where we simply talk about our lives and current events. There is another group that meets at my church where the topics usually are around more profound matters, like happiness, family life, or social justice. In the past, I have created groups discussing a particular philosophy like Taoism or The Law of Attraction.

Unfortunately, I had no idea I was about to be hit by a terrible set of challenges. A few weeks before the Coronavirus was declared a global pandemic, my father died of health complications due to old age. He was ninety-eight. He was a man who had touched many lives in our community. While this was hard for me, it wasn't unexpected. I wanted him to have a nice, traditional funeral. Sadly, we could not do so because COVID-19 restrictions were already in place. We finally buried his ashes more than a year later. By then, many of us had been vaccinated against the virus.

In March 2020, the American government declared a total lockdown, and life stopped. School, work, meetings, church, and other activities were done online or canceled. At that point, I started falling slowly into a dark hole of isolation and loneliness. As the daily death count increased, I sank deeper. Besides the isolation, I also felt depressed and overwhelmed by everything around me. It was an awful time for me. But fortunately, the COVID-19 vaccines came sooner than everyone had expected. And I remember watching TV on the morning of Dec 14, 2020, with tears in my eyes as a young nurse from New York received one of the first vaccines with a clear expression of relief on her face. At that moment, my only thought was getting my life back on track.

However, I found out immediately after the lockdown rules began to lift that getting back to my "normal" life was not easy. I could not seem to bounce back to my previous social life. But I did start taking baby steps to get myself out of that disconnected state. Then, as I began to emerge, I found more dark days yet to come for me. In the spring of 2021, I discovered lumps in several places in my body. As a breast cancer survivor, nothing causes panic like finding lumps! I was afraid that I was having a cancer relapse. Luckily, after several appointments, with many different doctors, they confirmed that I did not have a cancer relapse. All the anomalies were explained medically. Only one required surgery.

Ideally, this good news should have relieved me of my poor mental attitude. But it didn't. Eventually, I realized that the totality of the different traumatic events I had experienced during the past three years affected my mental health worse than I thought. Many things about me seemed fundamentally changed at that point.

The worst effect was that I had little desire to reconnect with anyone.

I knew I couldn't continue living such an isolated life. Fortunately, one of my friends reached out to me with support and companionship. I began to remember who I was before my withdrawal. Through conversation and her understanding, I became empowered to start my reconnection journey.

Like I did during childhood, I gathered my courage and began fighting my way out of my social isolation. I started having long conversations with my other friends and loved ones. Whether in-person, on the phone, or via Zoom, those conversations turned out to be my great lifesaver or mind-saver! I forced myself to leave my house for grocery shopping instead of ordering delivery. I went back to my exercising routine at the local YMCA. I purposely left my house every day to run minor errands or get a cup of coffee at the local coffee shop. As I became more comfortable, I attended public events like church services and family get-togethers again.

I have made progress in overcoming my struggle with social disconnection and isolation. I'm steadily getting stronger by participating in some of my former conversational groups and going out more socially. I accept that I have changed forever. I am coming to terms with this new version of myself. I believe I'm nearly back to where I once was in the company of others.

But, if you are currently going through a rough patch of social isolation and reluctance to build or rebuild solid and satisfying relationships with your loved ones or make new friends, I want you to know that you are not alone. Besides you and me, over 36% of the American populace also suffers from severe loneliness and social isolation. You may think, "Oh, but I have a very different set of circumstances that led me to this point." *Please understand that it doesn't matter what circumstances got you here, whether it had to do with health issues, the global pandemic, the death of a loved one, a job loss, divorce, or the ongoing upheaval in the world.* The most important thing is that you have completed the first and most crucial part of this transformation journey - bravely acknowledging that you want to break free from your cage of social isolation and transform your life for the better.

This book is reality-based guidance that can help you get your social life back on track. You and I will start this knowledge-seeking adventure by identifying and confronting the factors contributing to social hesitancy.

Then, we will analyze and review some of the necessary conversation skills to connect comfortably with others, whether they are family members, friends, or acquaintances.

Confidence is a critical element of any conversation. We will explore the best strategies for building confidence and self-esteem, enabling us to easily engage with new people and develop great friendships. We will also uncover the secret to finding or creating the most beneficial face-to-face conversational groups.

Ultimately, we all deserve the happiness and fulfillment of deep friendships and great relationships. You are just a few steps away from beginning a powerful transformational journey that holds the key to those benefits! All you need is the desire to start and the courage to take action. I hope you find your way out of disconnection as I am doing. I wish you the best of luck!

1

A CURRENT FEELING OF DISCONNECTION

"All You Have To Do Is Know Where You're Going. The Answers Will Come To You Of Their Own Accord."

— EARL NIGHTINGALE

Many people feel uncomfortable reconnecting with friends or making new friends.

Becoming someone that you barely recognize is confusing. I had changed from a person with close friends, deep, meaningful relationships with family members, and an active social life. I had changed into an unsocial, disconnected person living an isolated life. It wasn't easy to comprehend. I asked myself, "What is going on with me? Why do I feel disconnected from everyone and everything around me? How did I lose the sense of belonging that I once enjoyed? Where did this feeling of emptiness come from?"

Lots of similar questions might be running through your mind. Before we move on, pause and take a deep breath. In this chapter, we'll uncover some answers to these worrying questions. We'll unravel why we feel lost and disconnected from the people and activities we once loved. You'll find that those negative feelings are the natural progression of your thoughts about external things. And there is a natural way to exit those negative thought patterns.

WHY DO I FEEL THIS WAY?

After years of research, renowned psychologists have identified the three components of social isolation responsible for how you, me, and one-third of people worldwide feel. The three components are disconnection from self, social anxiety, and loneliness. Clearly, our feelings didn't appear out of the blue! Years of research cannot be wrong. Now that the components of social isolation have been identified let's look at each of them and see how they affect our current reality.

People May Feel Isolated for Several Reasons

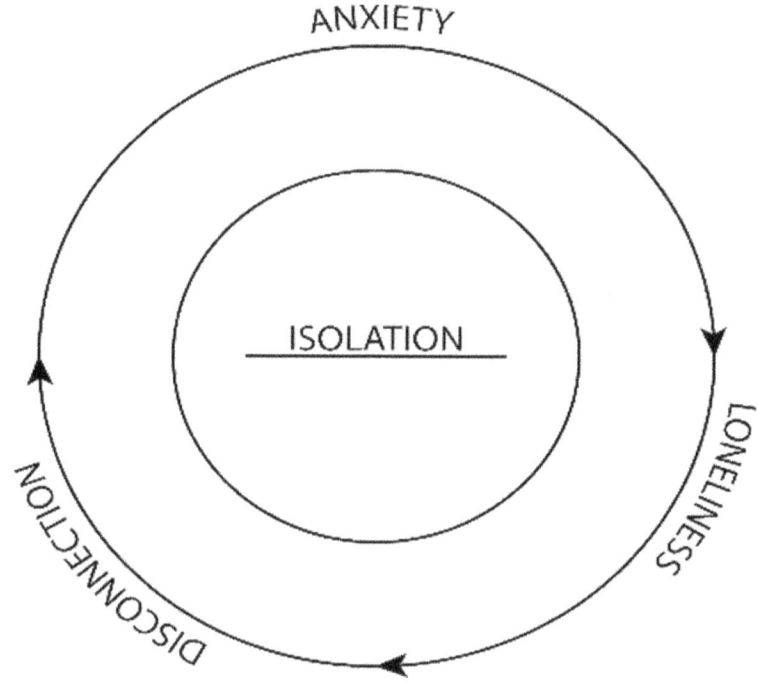

The common elements identified are disconnection within oneself, social anxiety, and pervasive loneliness.

1. Disconnection within Oneself

We've been raised to believe that the most important relationships in the world are those we have with our parents and siblings. Would you believe those aren't the most critical relationships in our lives? It's the truth. As humans, our most important relationship is with ourselves. The basis of our existence lies in deeply connecting with our inner self. To a large extent, that connection influences almost everything about life, including relationships with other people. Most importantly, it defines who we are.

What happens if that deep connection with the inner self is lost? Chaos – that's the perfect word to sum it all up. When we lose touch with our inner self, emptiness begins to creep in until it completely overtakes the mind. Our thoughts turn negative, and our mind becomes a battlefield. The constant clash between the negative self-talk and our true inner self creates a fissure that grows with each passing day. Soon, we've lost sight of our inner self, our life's meaning, and the very purpose for which we live. Once distanced from the essential relationship, the one with our inner self, chaos is what remains.

Chaos doesn't stop within the mind. It directly affects all parts of life. After emptiness has disconnected a person from their inner self, all meaningful family relationships, friendships, and social connections fall like dominos. Loved ones might feel like they don't know us anymore because the bond that connects them to us is broken and empty.

Several psychological studies have revealed that we instinctively disconnect to protect ourselves when trying to block out painful or traumatic events. Usually, this begins during childhood. The cycle starts because as children, we're not emotionally prepared to confront or process painful events, emotions, or experiences. These unprocessed experiences become the foundation of the disconnect from our inner self. So instead, we work hard to hide and suppress those emotions for as long as possible.

The feelings from long-forgotten painful experiences and traumatic events don't disappear if we leave them unprocessed. They remain pushed down under the weight of additional unresolved traumas. The longer that these feelings are unresolved, the more familiar and ingrained into our personalities they become. For some of us, it translates to emotional numbness. The constant emotional suppression leads to entirely disconnecting emotionally from ourselves. As we consider the years of painful memories and suppressed trauma, we understand how we have been entirely numbed by continuous emotional suppression.

Everyone has a different and unique story regarding trauma and pain and how this all works out for them. For some people, it could be a recent experience of physical or sexual abuse. Other people might have experienced the death of a loved one, the loss of a fulfilling job, or a significant breakup with their long-term partner. In my case, my social isolation story all began with my father's death. That was my starting point. From there, I continued to experience adverse circumstances for quite a while. Still, instead of adequately addressing those emotions, I unconsciously added them to my accumulated suppressed trauma. As a result, I was overwhelmed by the emotional overload, which triggered my particular social issues.

2. Increasing Social Anxiety

An unforeseen by-product of the pandemic lockdown was the number of people who developed social anxiety. Mental health agencies, including the World Health Organization, have stated that they have seen the number of people reaching out for help skyrocket. The primary reason that people are reaching out for help is that they feel anxious outside of their homes. It's not surprising that so many people are reaching out for help. Modern human beings derive a great deal of their identity from the relationships they create outside their home and their family units. For approximately twelve months, many of us stayed in the relative safety of our homes. Having little else to do, we watched hour upon hour of television. Newscasters, governmental officials, doctors, and average citizens were beamed into our homes on televisions, tablets, and laptops. Their sole purpose was to keep us up to date with facts, figures, and fear. Many of us sat transfixed while we absorbed the negativity and internalized our fear of an unknown and unseen enemy. For some people, our worst fears came true. A friend, coworker, or family member lost their life to COVID-19. Now that we're on the other side of the worst days of the pandemic and we essentially returned to our day-to-day routines, it's easy to see why so many of us are living with anxieties centered on returning to the new normal.

Before the pandemic, holiday gatherings, birthday parties, summer barbecues, family reunions, and weddings were happy celebrations that we anticipated and enjoyed. We looked forward to creating memories with friends and family members. During the pandemic, these gatherings were discouraged, and some states banned over ten people at outdoor gatherings.

When the pandemic restrictions on travel and gathering for celebrations with family and friends were removed, some of us became anxious simply thinking about meeting with friends for a hike or a meal. Attending a family gathering may cause physical symptoms such as excessive perspiration, a racing heart rate, or even shortness of breath. This is what social anxiety looks like in the post-pandemic world.

Psychologists describe this as re-entry social anxiety. Here is how it works; when we find ourselves back in social situations that we used to enjoy now, it feels very different, unfamiliar, and uncomfortable. Our body responds to our environment. The intensity and duration of these responses vary depending on the individual. These symptoms are genuine and meet the clinical definition of an anxiety attack. Many of us would rather forfeit any form of social activity, no matter how interesting it might sound, rather than go through that kind of physical reaction. However, by isolating and resisting all forms of in-person social interaction, we continuously lose more and more of our connection with our friends, family, and the rest of society.

3. Loneliness

Loneliness is a natural but complex human emotion. We frequently understand being lonely as physically separated from family and friends. However, it goes far beyond this average definition. I only understood this fact after reading a phenomenal book titled *Loneliness: Human Nature And The Need For Social Connection* by

Neuroscientists John T. Cacioppo and William Patrick. These two authors explore loneliness's scientific, biological, and social aspects. They also analyze the consequential damages loneliness can have on a person's overall health. I strongly recommend this book to everyone struggling with social disconnection and isolation.

As demonstrated in that book, there is a definite connection between social disconnection and loneliness. Loneliness isn't as straightforward as being sad about the lack of friends in one's life. It's an actual state of mind tied to social and physical disconnectedness. It carries an inescapable feeling of emptiness. A deep sense of loneliness begins when a person becomes aware of the disparity between the quality and quantity of social relationships one has and those one would like to have. There is a conflict that happens when a person lives with deep loneliness. Human beings have an instinctual need for companionship. Still, social and emotional disconnection is a barrier that makes satisfying that basic need impossible.

The inability to connect leaves a bitter and empty feeling. Those feelings worsen when family and friends go on happily socializing without us. One of the lies we tell ourselves is that neither our friends nor family would understand our loneliness, isolation, or disconnectedness. Choosing to join friends or family unlocks additional inner conflict. Being present with other people outwardly solves the solitary component of loneliness. The unseen parts of being disconnected, alone, and lonely remain. Often, feeling alone in a group of people leads to internalized guilt, a deep sense of shame, and increased negative self-talk that causes more profound, deeper resentment of self. We react by resenting ourselves more and then feeling ashamed.

But if deep loneliness goes beyond being alone or lacking physical proximity to people, what is the cause? Based on several studies, researchers and psychology experts have defined five additional factors that contribute massively to the development of human loneliness. Human beings are incredibly complex; internal and external forces add to our complexity. We have focused on inner complexities and conscious and unconscious choices that impact individual circumstances. These five factors are outside of personal choice and contribute to human loneliness. They are:

- Perceived Personal Inadequacies
- Unfulfilling Intimate Relationships
- Significant Separation or Relocation
- Social Marginality
- Developmental Delays and Social Skill Gaps

Let's look at how each of these may contribute to loneliness.

1. Perceived Personal Inadequacies

Personal inadequacies compromise the endless loop of negative self-talk narrating our daily lives. It comes from negative comments injected into our younger lives by parents, teachers, coaches, and other adults in positions of authority. Parents compare us to our siblings. Teachers compare us to classmates and siblings. Coaches compare us to teammates and previous team members. Here are some examples of things we may have in our negative self-talk file:

- "You got a B in math and a C in chemistry! Why can't you be smart, like your brother?"
- "I don't know why you're struggling with this formula. All of your classmates understand this. Maybe you don't belong in this class."
- "How did you miss that shot? Are you blind!?! Team, Dawson here just got you all 20 laps at practice tomorrow. Be sure to thank your teammate."
- "What makes you think that you're talented enough to play the lead in this production? You've never been on stage!"

- "Sweetie, you really need to set more reasonable goals for yourself. With your grades you'll never get into the school you want."
- "Face it, you're pretty but you're not a natural beauty like your mother. You just have to work at it a little harder."

Comments like these are internalized and take on new meanings. You're stupid. You're not talented. You don't belong here. You're not physically attractive. Year after year, comments like these chip away at our self-esteem, and we filter our opinion of ourselves through them, making us feel worthless.

Adverse childhood experiences affect our mindset severely. People who constantly perceive personal inadequacies may panic, waiting for others to respond with rejection or other adverse reactions. At this stage, loneliness begins to snowball. Since disconnection has a firm hold, there is no way to reach people with whom to connect. On the other hand, everyone else seems to socialize effortlessly. That's the peak stage of loneliness and not necessarily what you are going through!

2. Unfulfilling Intimate Relationships

Sexual intimacy is most likely the first thing that pops into your mind when you see the word "intimate." However, the most fulfilling, meaningful, and profound relationships don't develop through sexual intimacy but through non-sexual emotional and physical intimacy. To help us understand better, let's first analyze these two concepts.

Non-sexual emotional intimacy involves a person voluntarily expressing the deepest and most genuine parts of their lives to the people they trust. Those parts could be thoughts, emotions, secrets, fears, struggles, desires, and dreams. They could be either positive, negative, or even shameful. When emotional intimacy is shared with someone else, the other person doesn't judge but listens and offers unbiased reactions.

Most importantly, they accept the other person just the way they are. These interactions create closeness, comfort, safety, and friendship. Communication and feelings are not one-sided. Mutual trust develops, along with love, care, and respect, forming the foundation for high-level emotional intimacy.

Non-sexual physical intimacy involves the honest communication of personal and intimate feelings (described above) without expectations of those actions leading to sexually intimate activity. It may, however, involve physical closeness or touching. For example, when friends sit close together, hold hands to show support, or hug one another. Those actions would be non-sexual physical intimacy.

So, what about *intimate relationships* where there is a sexual expectation? Ideally, a sexual relationship would first be based on non-sexual intimacy. Without that basis, things can, and usually do, go wrong quickly. Non-sexual emotional and physical intimacy sounds perfect for any relationship. For many of us who have experienced or are in unfulfilling sexual relationships, this is how loneliness can exist within a relationship. When a relationship lacks the foundation of non-sexual emotional and physical intimacy, feelings of isolation develop. When one person in the couple is never available to listen to and tune in to the deepest feelings, desires, dreams, etc, of the other, resentment eventually develops. In addition, when there is no experience of those gentle non-sexual physical actions, it's impossible to build intimacy. Rather than feeling close, safe, and comfortable, the two people begin to feel distanced. Ultimately, that unfulfilled physical and emotional gap is filled with loneliness.

3. Significant Separation or Relocation

At some point in life, everyone experiences significant and sometimes unexpected loss. When someone very close is lost, that sense of connection is abruptly cut off. Such loss comes with intense emotional pain that makes a person want to withdraw from the rest of the world. Feelings of loneliness and isolation become dominant.

Death is not the only form of significant separation that can lead to social isolation. Sometimes, people become separated from close friends and relatives because of a long-distance job, divorce, immigration to a different country, or another long-term event.

Many people spend their entire lives within thirty miles of their childhood home. It's where family and friends also call home, and that small section of the world is all they know and trust. Isolation becomes a problem when a person leaves their familiar surroundings. It continues to be a problem until they acclimate to the new location.

Another instance of isolation and loneliness is among the elderly. Studies have shown that those feelings persistently increase among older adults in America, especially those aged 65 and above. According to renowned psychological researchers, older adults are particularly susceptible to isolation primarily because of health issues. Whether it's an issue of limited physical mobility, a hospital stay, or long-term care, elders experience significant separation from their loved ones. And, of course, the more they experience separation, the more intense their feelings of loneliness and social isolation become.

4. Social Marginality

America is probably one of the most democratic and wealthiest countries in the world. But American society operates with a system that does not uphold a culture of inclusivity. Many people who belong to minority groups are still denied access to certain rights, opportunities, infrastructure, and social services. Their exclusion may be based on gender, race, color, disabilities, and political beliefs.

For some, the cause of loneliness can be traced to the exclusion or marginalization experienced in school or at work. We might have experienced or observed students rejecting and excluding others from their social circle because of race, color, or disability. It could also be the same with adults in the workplace, where people are ostracized because of their background or other personal qualities. They may not be included in conversations, invited to office hangouts, or consulted for opinions on issues, even when those issues affect them directly. Ultimately, this social exclusion leaves that student or work team member with no friends at school or work.

The effects of social Marginality have the power to disrupt a person's mindset. As people continue to be excluded socially, they start to believe that there is something inherently wrong with them personally. As a result, they might deal with those situations by trying to protect themselves by becoming invisible to others.

But that social invisibility comes with the consequence of loneliness. Hiding in a shell, free from the rest of the prejudiced world, they desperately wish for connection. Fear of the negative impact of discriminatory actions stops them from approaching even the nicest-looking person in the office or making a connection with the one who does attempt to be friendly.

5. Developmental Deficits

This final factor outlined by the experts does not relate to our goal in this chapter or this entire book. But it should be acknowledged that the developmentally and physically impaired community members are often isolated. Their disabilities may make it very difficult for them to socialize, which is heartbreaking. Every effort should be made to include the physically or mentally disabled in society as much as possible. Many books have been written dealing with this type of isolation. Please investigate if you are interested.

AM I OKAY?

At this point, you might have begun to measure yourself against the causes of isolation and disconnection. Have you identified the primary causes of your disconnection and social isolation based on our defined factors? Are you wondering if your current mental condition is "normal" or is too complicated to address with a self-help book? To help solve that dilemma, let's quickly break down the differences between what is considered normal and not normal regarding a person's mental health.

What Is the Difference?

The first thing to know about mental health is that it sums up the state of our overall psychological wellness. Mental health includes thinking, relating to people, and regulating emotions. The World Health Organization (WHO) defines a person with normal mental health as "one who can cope with the typical stressors of life while still working to achieve their highest potential and contributing to their immediate community."

The state of normal mental health can vary from reasonable to poor. It depends on the degree to which external factors like stress, rejection, poor physical health, or traumatic experiences affect our daily lives. Mental health will most likely be lacking if we're going through a challenging period in life. We are considered to be in good mental health if we can improve our situation on our own or with the consultation of a professional mental health expert.

Mental health disorders or mental illnesses are much more complicated than poor normal mental health. Mental health disorders negatively affect how we think, feel, and relate to others. Its effects on our mental health are so intense that they significantly disrupt our ability to function.

Mental disorders are medically diagnosable with a standard set of criteria, signs, and symptoms developed by the American Psychiatric Association. The only person who can properly diagnose a mental health disorder is a psychiatrist, psychologist, or another mental health expert. Mental health professionals assess a person mentally and physically to see if they fulfill standard criteria for a specific mental health disorder. It is nearly impossible for non-professionals to make such a crucial diagnosis on their own because of the unique symptoms of each mental health disorder.

Now that we have the particular features of both conditions, we can see a significant difference between normal mental health and mental health disorders. "Normal" mental health affects all of us to varying degrees. In contrast, mental health disorders are specific to only those who have been professionally diagnosed. Nevertheless, recent research studies have revealed that people struggling with social disconnection and isolation are susceptible to two major mental health disorders. They are depression and anxiety. The levels of depression and anxiety are much more pronounced than we discussed previously.

Depression

Depression, as a mental health disorder, occurs at varying levels. It generally causes people diagnosed with depression to experience persistent and uncontrollable sadness and hopelessness. The symptoms of depression are more intense than occasional sadness. Instead, the symptoms include unexplainable physical exhaustion, extremely low moods, the inability to focus or concentrate, social withdrawal, and thoughts of suicide. In the worst cases of psychotic depression, a person may also experience hallucinations and delusions where they begin to see, hear or smell things that are unreal or are not present in their immediate surroundings.

Anxiety

It's important to note that the normal anxiety we experience daily differs from anxiety as a mental health disorder. This form of anxiety is a disorder all on its own; it can also be a symptom of depression. Anxiety disorder causes a person to experience persistent and excessive levels of worry, restlessness, and irritability. Its other symptoms include panic attacks, unexplainable fatigue, muscle stiffness, social phobia, inability to concentrate, insomnia, and other sleep problems.

If you suspect that you are showing these severe symptoms of either depression or anxiety, it would be best to consult a mental health expert for a proper diagnosis. The symptoms of depression and anxiety listed above indicate treatable mental health disorders. Please consult a medical or mental health professional for appropriate diagnosis and symptom management. Suppose the diagnosis turns out to be positive. In that case, your mental health provider can recommend suitable treatment options, whether in the form of medications, psychotherapy, brain stimulation therapies, or relaxation techniques. Ultimately, early diagnosis and treatment go a long way in helping people overcome any mental health disorder.

In 2022, 19.86% of adults in the USA experienced mental health struggles. Equivalent to nearly 50 million

Americans. 4.91% experienced a severe mental illness. The prevalence of adults with a major depressive episode is highest among individuals between 18 and 25. Depression is among the most treatable mental disorders. Between 80% and 90% of people with depression respond well to treatment.

People with mental health struggles often experience stigma or discrimination. Stigma is a mark of disgrace associated with a particular circumstance. There is absolutely no disgrace related to having any form of mental illness. Judgment and the opinions of others almost always stem from a lack of understanding rather than information based on facts. Helping educate others can make a big difference. There should be no more stigma attached to mental health issues than any other illness. Family, friends, clergy, or community members can offer support if they are aware of a diagnosis of mental illness. Reach out to those you trust for compassion, support, and understanding.

It's important for all of us, not just those who deal with mental health issues, to cultivate hope when faced with depression and anxiety. Research shows that hope and mental health are inextricably linked. Hope helps to moderate the impact of depression and anxiety. One way to become more hopeful is to focus on our strengths. Remembering and using our strengths creates confidence that we can get through whatever comes our way.

We can strengthen hope by taking small, daily actions to help us thrive amidst uncertainty. We can practice gratitude. At the end of every day, think back on three things for which to be grateful. We can also reframe negative thoughts. For example, change the idea "I'm never going to stop feeling anxious about everything that's going on" to "It's natural to be anxious right now, and there are things I can do to make it better." Every positive thought builds hope and expectation for a brighter future.

Those suffering from what doctors refer to as post-acute sequelae of COVID-19, PASC, or "Long COVID," may be interested in several effective drugs. These drugs treat depression, fatigue, and the physical symptoms associated with these unique health problems. Please speak with your healthcare professional if you have not already been offered these medications. Some statistics show them to be very effective.

I encourage you to seek help if you feel you need it. Whatever your determination of your current mental state, whether it's reasonable or more serious, this book should not be used as a substitute for diagnosable problems. There should be no fear or shame in seeking medical advice or treatment for any mental health problem or disorder.

In the following chapters of this book, we will explore several highly effective techniques to improve social interaction skills and help manage social withdrawal. If you are seeing a therapist currently, you can mention this book to them and suggest that it contains some subjects for discussion. Topics in this book could add to the benefits of your therapy sessions.

On that positive note, we will begin building some stepping stones toward reconnection to social activity.

YOU CAN TALK TO ANYONE
TO BREAK OUT OF ISOLATION

2

POSITIVE HEALTH BENEFITS OF BEING WITH OTHERS

"You may Say I'm a Dreamer, But I'm Not the Only One. I Hope Some Day You'll Join Us. And the World Will Live as One."

— JOHN LENNON

Being Socially Active Is Good for You!

The first thing we need to look at is our mindset. The Oxford Dictionary defines mindset as "a habitual or characteristic mental attitude that determines how you will interpret and respond to situations." The words "Habitual...

mental attitude" could be replaced with "habit of thought." A habit is any set of behaviors that becomes routine. We know habits can be changed with practice. The goal here is to build positive habits of thought about regaining social connection.

To overcome social disconnection, we need to tweak the mindset that controls it. Step 1 is to make a list of all our current thoughts or reasons that we avoid the activities we used to enjoy. Take a few minutes to get in touch with thoughts about social reluctance. This is a process that will take a bit of consideration and effort. Many people find it helpful to write down their thoughts and feelings. You may want to dedicate a notebook or a journal to this exercise. It will be great to look back at it to see progress. If you hate doing this kind of thing, don't worry, you have other choices. You don't absolutely need to write anything down. You can keep an imaginary list in mind. If typing on your computer is a better option, several journaling apps are available. Some are free. Search for them on the internet. Journal writing is my way of organizing my thoughts. Any way that works for you is just fine.

Do you have a good-sized list? Do you have five or more items? Next to each one, write - or imagine - something that feels just one step better. When the new list is set up, take a look at it. These better-feeling items are going to become your new mindset.

The next step in this exercise is to be willing to read - or say to yourself - the new list at least once a day until it becomes a habit. For example, whenever you start thinking, "I just don't feel like going out," immediately follow it with, "I'm going out anyway." Or, "I'm going out at (*add a specific time*)." You can be as creative as you like with your replacement thoughts as long as they're positive and move you forward to your goal of becoming more outgoing. If you tell yourself to leave your house at a specific time, then make sure you keep to your plan!

Here is some information I found on the internet regarding forming a new habit:

Maxwell Maltz was a plastic surgeon in the 1950s when he began noticing a strange pattern among his patients. When Dr. Maltz performed an operation — like a nose job, for example — he found that it would take the patient about 21 days to get used to seeing their new face. Similarly, when a patient had an arm or a leg amputated, Maxwell Maltz noticed that the patient would sense a phantom limb for about 21 days before adjusting to the loss of the limb.

These observations prompted Maltz to consider his adjustment period to changes and new behaviors. He noticed that it also took him about 21 days to form a new habit. Maltz wrote about these experiences and said, "These, and many other commonly observed phenomena tend to show that it requires a minimum of about 21 days for an old mental image to dissolve and a new one to gel." In 1960, Maltz published that quote and his other thoughts on behavior change in a book called Psycho-Cybernetics which is now an audiobook. When he published the physical book, it became a blockbuster hit, selling more than 30 million copies.

Twenty-one days is a relatively short time, though other psychologists suggest a more extended period. The old mindset was solidly in place. Getting the new one to be your dominant thought will take some work. The best way to practice is to keep writing (or thinking) the new replacement thoughts whenever you feel the old thought pattern taking over.

You'll know you have successfully established your more positive thoughts when you no longer need to make a conscious substitution. Your new positive mindset is in place. Whatever time it takes will be worth the effort. Establishing a mindset is the beginning of all conscious change.

If you did start writing a list and you think a journal is a good idea, that's great! Writing helps people see their thoughts and feelings and measure progress toward new beliefs and habits. This book will present more opportunities to write down your thoughts and ideas.

To reinforce the new mindset, we will examine the positive health benefits of being active socially. Notice that the old mindset was a stumbling block. It prevented you from moving forward. The new and improved version is a stepping stone that will move you forward. Your old mindset blocked you whenever you tried to gain the courage to overcome your fear. The new mindset will support you in whatever you choose to do.

In the rest of this chapter, we will examine some life skills and practical tips you can incorporate into your daily life to break that cycle of isolation. You deserve to reactivate your social life as soon as possible. We will reinforce the new positive mindset by discussing the benefits of being socially active.

THE HEALTH BENEFITS OF SOCIAL CONNECTIONS

We know that things like eating nutritious meals, exercising regularly, getting adequate quality sleep, and getting regular medical checkups keep us healthy. An often overlooked part of a healthy lifestyle is strong social connections.

As humans, we are born with an inherently powerful desire to connect socially with other people. We're social animals. We cannot help but yearn to build relationships and experience a sense of belonging and closeness. Socialization is a fundamental part of our human nature. It is not surprising that constantly connecting with others improves the quality of our lives in all ways. Several research studies prove this. A rich and active social life offers many positive benefits to our physical, emotional, and mental health.

1. Boosts Quality of Life and Increases Lifespan

Today, we live in a fast-paced world that interferes with physical wellness. An erratic lifestyle can interfere with health. All the things we deal with, like working hard to pay bills, raising children, perhaps going to school ourselves, and trying to achieve life goals, cause immense stress. Disregarding the impact of long-term stress harms our bodies.

The combination of physical stress and social isolation leads to the increased production of cortisol. This toxic stress hormone weakens the immune system. It also makes us susceptible to chronic health conditions like high blood pressure and heart disease. These chronic conditions affect the quality of life and shorten the life span.

Medical experts and scientific researchers have verified that the health benefits are enormous when we're part of a solid social network. When social interaction is as essential as exercising and healthy eating habits, our quality of life is upgraded. The chances of longevity increase by 50%.

Consistent cortisol release in the body causes adverse effects on the immune system. Taking time to interact and connect with others does the opposite. Consistent interaction and connection with other people improves health. This benefit works when we socialize both within and outside our social circle. According to medical experts, simple social activities like hanging out with friends, spending time and having dinner with your family, or even hugging your children lead to increased good hormone levels in the body, specifically oxytocin.

Oxytocin, popularly known as the love hormone, reduces the adverse effects of stress by slowing the production and release of cortisol. The significant reduction prevents our immune system from breaking down and becoming susceptible to chronic illnesses. People with chronic pain due to arthritis, fibromyalgia, or Lyme disease also benefit from oxytocin's pain-relieving and calming traits.

In the hustle and bustle of the modern world, there are enclaves of people seemingly unaffected by stress, loneliness, or poor health. One group of people who caught the attention of researchers is the residents of Sardinia, an island off the coast of Italy. In 2019, Harvard's School of Public Health conducted several studies on Sardinians' unusual longevity. The experts found that the secret to the healthiness and longevity of the Sardinian population lies in the strong ties they share with their family and friends. The findings showed that these people participated in strenuous physical activities as well. The experts emphasized that their firm social connection significantly affects their long lifespan. We have access to similar kinds of benefits as the population of Sardinia. All it takes is the ability to restore and reawaken our social activity.

2. Improves Mental Health

In the last chapter, we looked at normal mental health. A consistent lifestyle of social connection can help lessen the impact of depression and anxiety. The positive benefits of a social network counteract the adverse effects of exhaustion or traumatic experience. By maintaining healthy social connections, people with depression and anxiety have access to emotional support, hope for the future, and inspiration to continue positive relationships: self-esteem and a sense of worthiness increase.

Researchers in Buffalo, New York, studied over 300 men and women who used free health clinics. The study found that the people with the highest and most consistent level of social connection were the least likely to suffer from anxiety and depression. The sense of belonging that comes with genuine social connections produces a feeling of security. Ultimately, we feel more encouraged to approach others, start conversations, and build friendships.

3. Stimulates Better Memory.

As we grow older, we are bound to become more forgetful because of age-related decline. While interacting with different people, we engage our memory skills as much as we exercise our language abilities. A function of memory called "Cognitive Reserve" comes into play. Cognitive reserve refers to how tasks are performed. It is believed to cause some people to be more resilient than others.

Cognitive reserve is built or accumulated in several ways. A healthy brain in a stimulating environment grows new cells and builds cognitive reserve by making new neural connections. Studies show a positive link between having an active social and intellectual life throughout the adult years and a decreased risk of cognitive decline in later years. A healthy, well-developed brain resists the effects of injury from trauma or stroke or compromise associated with diseases such as diabetes, high blood pressure, or depression.

The concept of cognitive reserve holds out the promise of interventions that could slow cognitive aging or reduce the risk of dementia. Even in our 40s, 50s, and 60s, cognitive reserve helps keep memory and other cognitive abilities sharp. Although there is no way to prevent the body and brain from aging normally, accumulated "cognitive reserve" helps to mitigate the effects of aging, especially in terms of memory decline.

Another study found evidence to confirm that social interaction improves human memory. Researchers carried out a 15 to 18-month study using aging mice. The study grouped the mice in different ways. They housed some mice in batches of pairs and put other mice into groups of over six. Eventually, after being housed for about three months, the mice were subjected to different memory recall tests. The researchers discovered that all groups of mice had impressive memory recall abilities. The six or more mice housed together were better at observing and remembering things faster than their 'pair-housed' counterparts. Assuming that we can transfer mouse behavior to humans, the result of this study confirmed that social connection could stimulate memory skills. The researchers particularly emphasized that this memory stimulation increases as our social network or circle enlarges. In other words, the more we interact with new people and build social relationships with them, the better our memory skills will become.

4. Lower Risk Factors for Dementia.

Memory impairment is not the only problem that comes with aging. As people age, there is an increased risk of developing Alzheimer's disease and other forms of dementia. Alzheimer's disease is currently the most common type of dementia in the United States. As of 2020, there are over five million elderly Americans affected by Alzheimer's. In the next thirty years, the number of Alzheimer's patients is expected to balloon to more than thirteen million. Dementia involves a massive decline in a person's overall cognitive functioning abilities. It includes severe symptoms like total memory loss and the inability to complete daily tasks like bathing, dressing, driving, or cooking. The deterioration includes hallucinations, delusions, visual impairment, and severe depression.

Scientists have discovered that social connection can be a protective barrier between older adults and the development of different dementia types. Dementia develops when an abnormal build-up of a particular protein known as Interleukin-6 or IL-6 collects in specific brain areas. These areas are associated with memory, learning, and other cognitive abilities. It takes years for this protein to accumulate to an elevated level, where it begins to create problems. Research has revealed that social isolation and disconnection are significant factors that contribute to increased IL-6 levels in the brain.

Older adults should be encouraged to socialize as much as possible and maintain social relationships. They need increased opportunities to interact with peers, friends, children, grandchildren, and other loved ones. Staying connected is essential. Doing so will help ensure that lower levels of the IL-6 proteins are produced and accumulated in the brain.

YOU ALREADY HAVE EVERYTHING YOU NEED TO GET STARTED!

Social connection can improve physical, mental, and emotional well-being. Your perspective about social contact with friends and family is hopefully opening up. All that's left is to overcome your fears and reactivate your social lifestyle. The question in your mind may be, how and where do I begin?

Despite our extended period in social isolation, we never lost any social connection skills; they're just a little rusty. These are the same skills we began developing in childhood and built upon as we matured. Social skills don't grow in a vacuum. They're the result of contributions from agents of socialization. Sounds complicated, doesn't it? Let's look at this in simple terms. When we were young, every time we talked with people who had more developed social skills than us, they contributed to our social skills. Who are these amazing agents? Parents, teachers, older siblings, and coaches are typical examples of socialization agents.

The life skills we learned have enabled us to interact effortlessly with others in the past. Our social isolation phase caused us to lose confidence in our skills. It seems more difficult now to exercise them. It's time for a gentle reminder of what those social skills are.

Communication Skills

Communication skills are central to building, developing, and maintaining strong friendships and social relationships. If you think back to every friend you made in kindergarten, high school, or college, communication skills played a significant role in fostering those relationships. People aren't born with communication skills. We build them through consistent practice as we grow. However, when social isolation, depression, and anxiety set in, exercising our communication skills became difficult. We can reawaken our skills using the same consistent practice method we employed while growing up. Practice communicating with those closest to you as much as possible. As you keep practicing, you will become more comfortable and natural during conversations with other people. I noticed this myself. In my pre-pandemic life, I could talk effortlessly with nearly anyone. Now, I find myself searching for words and not coming across as clearly as I would like. It's an effort for me to speak up and speak out. Right now, I'm in the same place as you!

Communication skills include more than just initiating and maintaining conversations with others. Verbal cues that help others understand our spoken language are tone, intonation, rate, and word choice. Humans also rely on nonverbal cues to understand spoken language. We rely on eye contact, facial expression, and body language. We use speech, assertiveness, and non-verbal cues every time we communicate. Ultimately, rediscovering and developing our communication skills can go a long way in helping to overcome social anxiety. Feeling anxious talking with others is decreased when communication skills are dusted off and used regularly. When we know we have adequate communication skills, we are more confident.

Critical Thinking

Besides communication skills, our critical thinking ability is another essential skill that enables us to form a genuine social connection with others. The Oxford Dictionary defines critical thinking as "the objective analysis and evaluation of an issue in order to form a judgment." In other words, think before speaking or acting! The ability to think critically helps in the evaluation of the topics that are being discussed. Critical thinking helps form genuine connections with others as we listen to speakers and reply openly and thoughtfully. It becomes more crucial when reconnecting with friends after a long period of social isolation. Here again, I find myself a little rusty. I sometimes second-guess myself. I wonder what the other person's real motives are in some situations. I have to remind myself to give my friends the benefit of the doubt and keep myself from becoming offended.

When I start questioning the situation, I try to step back and not react immediately. More interaction is better than less, so I continue practicing my critical thinking skills. I'm remembering to be open to whatever is going on. I'm improving at assessing social situations and determining the best approach.

Imagine a time when you are chatting with a close friend you recently reconnected with, and the conversation begins to take a turn that makes you uncomfortable or anxious. If you feel inclined, take a few moments to journal about a situation like this. What kind of uneasy situation would it be for you? What other description could you use beyond feeling "uneasy"? What would your reaction be? What could you do or say in that situation? Let critical thinking skills swing into action in your imaginary problematic situation and help you devise different solutions. Some possible actions might be making an evasive move and turning the conversation from an uncomfortable subject to something else. Or you could end the conversation without making the other party feel insulted. There are ways to handle the situation. You handled conversations efficiently before, and you can do it again. You always have had that critical thinking ability to help you overcome challenges without increasing anxiety or fear.

Take the Other Person's Perspective

Empathy is crucial in social interaction. If we're lucky, we have had teachers and parents who instilled in us a sensitivity to other people. They taught us to filter our speech to ensure we do not hurt anyone's feelings. Thinking of the other person is the basis of empathy.

When we grow up and connect socially with people outside our family, we automatically try to be considerate of the other person's feelings. I clearly remember when I wanted to speak rudely to a friend. In my mind, I heard my mother's voice say, "If you can't say something nice, don't say anything at all!" Remember the art of considering the other person's perspective. Getting this skill back could be as easy as taking the interaction slowly for a while.

Here's an example. You might have friends who can't help but question why you have neglected them. In their opinion, there seems to be no reason for your continued isolation. You might be tempted to react negatively. Here's where taking it slowly helps. It may be that they didn't mean to insult you. They might have genuine concerns about your well-being and want to know what's happening with you. By considering the emotions and feelings of others, you'll find it easier to hold back your initial reactions. You will be able to respond to them with an honest answer and not offend them. Or you could change the subject. It depends on your preference.

Focus on People and Make Connections

Social interaction and connection are always two-way processes. To engage effectively with our friends, family, and even strangers, we need to pay attention when other people are talking. Pay attention and listen to their verbal and nonverbal cues so we can respond appropriately. Before we isolated ourselves, these skills used to come quickly and naturally. It has been a while since these skills have been used outside of a virtual meeting. It's no surprise they need a dusting before they work flawlessly. We must reawaken the ability to focus on others to make the proper connection. When we can focus our minds on the person we're talking with, it becomes easier to forget about our fears and anxiety.

Here is another opportunity to reflect and write in your journal. Imagine stepping into a party with many people all talking and socializing. No doubt, this would trigger some social anxiety. In your mind, focus on just one person. Engage and interact with that one person. A smooth conversation with this person puts you at ease. In no time, you find yourself being introduced to more people and interacting with them without any form of awkwardness or hesitation. Based on this daydream, what are your thoughts about coming into the room, seeing everyone there, and choosing someone with whom to talk? Of all the people present, who would you like to speak with? What would you talk about? What are you comfortable sharing with them?

PRACTICAL TIPS TO BREAK THE CYCLE OF SOCIAL DISCONNECTION

I am walking the same path you are currently on. Trying to rebuild social skills after seemingly losing them is a challenge. Please be assured that you have everything it takes to beat this challenge and regain your social abilities. The exercise suggested above will help once you take a bold step and break your mind from its current negative cycle. Here's a chance to add some bricks to our positive mindset construction. It's the same exercise we used to break the habit of negative thoughts holding us back. Now we're going to expand it a little more. In your notebook or your mental list, find a better description of any resistant thoughts regarding associating with people socially. Try these thoughts out, but feel free to make a list of your own.

OLD MINDSET	NEW MINDSET
Changing the way I have been is tough.	I'm going to take it slowly at first.
I'm so out of practice at being with people.	It doesn't matter! It's better for me physically to do this.
I think I've lost my voice when it comes to holding a conversation.	I can and will be better at it with practice.
What if I have a panic attack?	That's crazy! I've never reacted like that before. I'll put all my focus on the other person.
What if I start to feel criticized?	I'll imagine that the other person is awkward. And they are just not expressing themselves well. What they want to show is a concern for me.
I get very anxious at parties. Maybe I won't go.	I'll limit myself to focusing on just one person and see how it goes. I'll leave whenever I choose.

These replacement thoughts won't come automatically. They have to be practiced. Whenever I catch myself falling back into a negative thought pattern, I consciously switch it to a more positive feeling thought.

New negative thoughts tend to bubble up as soon as some have been replaced with positive ones. One difference is that now you may notice that the negative thoughts are getting specific. There's more of a "What if…" flavor to it. This is a good sign because it shows that you imagine yourself in public, associating with other people. Take it one step further in your imagination and see yourself calm and at ease in that situation. See yourself handling it successfully. I have to keep working on this all the time. It's a little bit like playing Whack-A-Mole with negativity. Stay on the lookout for new negative thoughts and try to counteract them asap.

Here are more practical suggestions:

Intentionally Reconnect with Loved Ones.

Of course, fears will spring up and try to stop us from proceeding. However, we can take charge and silence these negative thoughts. Remember those close family members and friends who value and miss you. Remember that they never gave up but constantly reached out to you despite your noticeable withdrawal from them. It would help to also remember the joy, happiness, fulfillment, and positive health benefits that social connections can restore. We can take a step outside our comfort zone and begin this journey of reconnection. Silencing fear and doubt means replacing them with positive thoughts. Getting our old life back or an improved version of it will feel like taking the next logical step.

Start Small and Set Realistic Goals.

Take it gradually, at your own pace, to come out of your comfort zone and begin this social reconnection process. But resist the urge to retreat! A small step forward is better than no step at all. Recording positive actions in your journal or mental tabulations will help you keep going. Seeing progress right in front of you, in writing, helps to make it so! I really believe this.

Start small by establishing simple and short-term goals with dates attached. For example, pick a person to contact in one week. As confidence grows, move the time to a month, and list more people to contact. If there is a major holiday coming up, set some goals to accomplish before Thanksgiving or Christmas. Make a short list of family members and friends you want to contact before the holiday. You don't have to meet everyone in person. Connect some of them through text, email, or social media platforms like Facebook, Whatsapp, or Zoom calls. Get more comfortable using these means of communication. Then slowly move to in-person meetings with everyone if that seems right. Start accepting invitations to family dinners, social gatherings, or friendship hangouts if they come your way. It doesn't have to be every time they get together. Try attending once a month, and who knows? You might get comfortable enough to meet with them weekly or have a daily conversation.

When I started my social reconnection journey, I set up Zoom meetings with only a few of my close friends and family. During those meetings, we never talked about my problems or why I isolated myself from everybody else. Instead, we just talked about simple things, shared stories, and laughed over some of our silly experiences. Gradually, I was able to proceed to meet them in person. I slowly regained the sense of belonging and acceptance I used to enjoy whenever I was around them.

Start with whatever simple goals that you consider to be most achievable. This isn't supposed to be a fast track to freedom. It's a step along the journey. Nobody knows you better than yourself. Be realistic! If you know that setting a goal of meeting over ten people at once right away is not feasible for you now, please wait to do it. Doing too much too fast is overwhelming.

Focus On the External Environment.

After spending time in social isolation and situational depression, our minds automatically become trained to focus only on our inner thoughts without noticing what's happening around us. This trait can be frustrating because others misinterpret the lack of concentration as uncaring or rude. It's possible to overcome this by learning a mindfulness technique.

Start this exercise by finding a quiet place and sitting peacefully for 2 to 5 minutes. As you sit, try to focus on the present moment and not drown in your thoughts or worries. Sit on your porch or another outside area if it's in a comfortable, quiet space. Inside is fine too. Observe everything around you, from the color of the sky to the breeze blowing the trees and the birds flying by. If you're inside, gaze out a window or a picture on your wall. Concentrate on your breath while focusing your attention outside of yourself. Slowly inhale and exhale while keeping count of your inhalations and exhalations. Continue counting breaths until you get to 10 or 20. Focusing outward will have the effect of connecting you to the broader world.

This mindfulness exercise is the most basic form of meditation. It can have magical effects in unburdening and calming the mind. The best part is that you can practice it many times throughout the day because it only takes a short time. The more you practice it, the more you can gain complete control of your mind rather than allowing it to push you into being lost in thoughts. If you've never tried this technique before and like it, please explore it further. Many books, audiobooks, recordings, and live meditation sessions are easy to find on the internet or at the local bookstore.

Ultimately, when you find yourself around people, you will easily be able to notice particular things about them. You could initiate conversations by making observations or compliments about their looks, outfits, or other outer features. Throughout the conversation, you will be able to stay focused and give appropriate responses.

Be Compassionate with Yourself.

We are our own worst enemies and harshest critics. We often judge ourselves for not doing enough when we are actually trying our best. On our journey of social reconnection, we will also struggle with inner self-criticism more often than usual.

Take time to reflect on progress because this journey is challenging! We must remember to celebrate accomplishments and affirm the smallest amount of progress toward our goals as meaningful. Give yourself accolades for challenging your fears and picking up your phone to call and interact with that one friend you haven't been in touch with for a while. It doesn't matter if it was just one person you called throughout the day or if the conversation lasted only 5 minutes. The most important thing is overcoming the fear that prevented you from reaching out. Breaking that cycle of social disconnection is in your control now. You did it, so please take pride in yourself. Make an entry in your journal if you're writing.

There will be plenty of times when stumbling blocks and obstacles arise, and goal achievement is just beyond our grasp. We might not always achieve the social goals we set. Maybe we thought the plan was realistic but needed more courage to go through with it. For instance, you set a goal of attending your high school reunion at the end of the month. You prepared yourself mentally and emotionally for days. But when the day finally arrived, you couldn't do it. You dressed up nicely, but before you stepped outside your door, your fear and anxiety convinced you to stay home because seeing a large group of people was overwhelming.

When a goal is not achieved, try not to beat yourself up over it. It's important to stay positive. Shift your attention to the next event. In fact, it's normal to have setbacks. Be compassionate with yourself. Readjust your goals and look forward to achieving the next thing on your list.

Based on our exploration and the exercises we have outlined, rebuilding social connections is more realistic and manageable than previously believed. The health benefits of a life filled with social activity are well-researched, and that alone should provide motivation to continue the journey toward being more social. Your friends and family miss you. They will be happy to have you back in their company. You can kick loneliness aside because you have everything you need, plus the support of your loved ones, who will always cheer you on. Next, we will add to our social skills by dusting off our conversational abilities and discovering why conversation is the basis of connection.

YOU CAN TALK TO ANYONE
TO BUILD A CONNECTION

3

PROVEN CONVERSATION TECHNIQUES TO HELP YOU CONNECT

"Sometimes the Greatest Adventure Is Simply a Conversation."

— UNKNOWN

Brush up on some of the ways to navigate conversations and put them into practice.

Effective conversation is the best and most common way to connect with people. I think of that exchange as "currency," like money. It is exchanged between 2 or more people, enriching some and leaving others poorer. Conversation is a give-

and-take transaction, just like trading money for goods or services. The only difference is the participants in the transaction trade ideas, opinions, or thoughts. Ideally, all parties leave the conversation feeling equally rewarded, but that only happens sometimes. Some may feel more enriched than others, or some may feel unchanged or neutral. This may be one reason positive conversations leave us feeling enriched, and we feel a deficit when we haven't spoken with friends for a while or when the conversation is negative.

I don't think any studies have been done concerning this, or maybe they just haven't called it Social Currency. A brief search didn't yield any results using that term. I'm sure scientists would want to study many additional areas. For instance, highly emotional conversations, arguments, and discussions where there are issues of dominance or hierarchy, like at work, would be of interest. I can't find any scientific backup. There is plenty of neuroscientific information about what happens within our brains that causes pleasurable reactions during conversations. But I can't find anything that supports my ideas about currency. If appropriate, you have my permission to present this idea as your own. Let's see what people think about it. You can contact me via my Facebook page: https://www.facebook.com/profile.php?id=100086753341037

A vital way to achieve connection with others is to develop excellent conversation skills. Starting or maintaining a conversation after a long-term withdrawal is challenging. This difficulty can be overcome. Starting a conversation may feel awkward after being away from social opportunities. It's a normal phenomenon that almost everyone experiences in this situation. Just the act of speaking takes some warming up. I need to cough or clear my throat, or I'll croak like a frog!

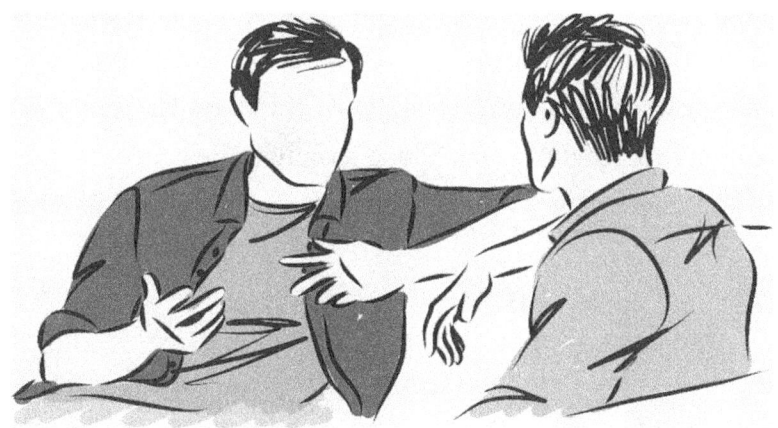

TRIED AND TRUE CONVERSATION SKILLS

Even if your voice croaks or creaks a little, you already have some background information about conversation mechanics. We've all been in conversations before, and there will be more talking to do in the future. This isn't new information; it's a review. The following suggestions are techniques that most experts agree are successful.

First, we want to understand what type of conversation we will have. Knowing what the social setting will be ahead of time is a good idea. If, for example, you are meeting an individual for the first time. You should discover a few things about them without making yourself or them uncomfortable. Or, what if you are reconnecting with a longtime friend and want to ask about their personal life? These two approaches would be entirely different. You might be cautious with strangers or someone you don't know. With someone you have known for a while, it's okay to be more direct.

- ***Cultivate Effective Communication***

One-on-one or small group conversations don't need a formal speechmaker. Short complete sentences will do. A common rule is the KISS concept, Keep it Short and Simple. (You thought it stood for something else, didn't you?) The point is that you don't have to make it a long, flowery speech. You could even mentally rehearse whatever you want to say before speaking out loud. A little mental run-through will eliminate filler words like "um" or "ah," too. Just ensure that what you say will make sense to the other person. Going slowly and simply will keep you calm and confident.

- *Master Information Branching*

Information branching involves providing information on a particular topic and then allowing the conversation to continue in another direction. Let's say you went to a dinner party with a friend and are asked what your favorite meal is. Instead of answering, "My favorite meal is steak and French fries," you could expand a little. For instance, give a response like, "Steak and French fries have been my favorite meal since childhood. It was the first meal I learned how to prepare myself. I'm pretty good at it now." With this response, you not only mentioned your favorite meal, but you also provided more information about yourself. This response invites others to add more details to many topics. They could branch the conversation to meal prep, their early cooking experiences, or which meals they prepare well.

Information branching keeps the conversation lively and keeps things moving. Suppose your audience or the other person is also a good communicator. In that case, they will keep the conversation going with more give-and-take branching, which maintains the flow of the conversation.

But what if you run out of things to say? Then it's perfectly okay to say," It was nice meeting you (or seeing you again)," and move on.

- ***Build Rapport***

Rapport (pronounced rap-pore') means a close and harmonious relationship in which the people or groups concerned understand each other's feelings or ideas and communicate well. You have no rapport when you meet a person for the first time. Rapport is built over time. Start building rapport by being friendly, offering a firm handshake and a smile, maintaining solid eye contact, and remembering the person's name. You want the other person to relate to you using verbal and nonverbal cues. Let them know that you are an understanding and trustworthy person through your actions and what you say.

When meeting a new person, it's essential to avoid being rude. Imagine sitting in a coffee shop, and someone you don't know sits next to you. You smile. They begin asking you questions. They never make eye contact or give their name; they just keep asking questions. Several days later, you cross paths with this person again. How do you handle the encounter? You would probably avoid the person because you came to the conclusion that they are rude and off-putting. Now, imagine the first encounter with the stranger differently. What if the meeting begins with the person introducing himself, and they shake your hand, smiling, and asking to sit with you? They ask some neutral questions and wait for your replies: "How do you like this weather?" "Is this the best coffee shop in this neighborhood?" "Is there a daily special?" "What do you recommend I order?" Would this change your response to the second chance encounter? You might like the opportunity to meet a new person and possibly make a new friend. The second imaginary encounter is the better way.

If you are the one who is new to the neighborhood, start slow and see if a rapport or connection happens. Watch for the other person's reaction and response to your words. Are they smiling? Are they glancing directly at you? If so, then you're most likely building rapport, a connection. You'll notice that some people are more receptive than others. This is human nature. If the magic isn't happening, feel free to move on and see if you can more easily build rapport with someone else. Sometimes a little conversation develops into a great connection.

People like to talk about themselves, but dislike being questioned, especially if the questions are personal. Personal questions make the other person feel uneasy and uncomfortable. Questions should be very neutral and have a purpose. Minus the questions, when you approach an individual and give an opinion about things that might interest them or even about yourself, you make it easy for them to share their thoughts.

Imagine a situation where a new person at work walks up to you and asks about your marriage. You'd be offended. She doesn't have to know this! It's perfectly acceptable to dodge the question and avoid the person. On the other hand, if she had approached you, said something admiring about your outfit, and asked an impersonal question, you would most likely respond positively. Rapport building paves the way for a good conversation without causing stress. Building a connection requires a little rapport first.

- **Use Storytelling**

Everyone likes to hear an interesting or exciting story. Storytelling is one of the quickest tricks you can use to build a connection with anyone. Do you recall a story you've come across lately? What kept you reading or listening till the very end? You were most likely captivated and ready to stick with it to know what happened at the end.

Stories can even connect you with a total stranger. You can start your conversation and build the connection you want when you've already captured attention with your story. Storytelling is a good starting point if there's a particular person with whom you would love to connect. But make sure the story is related to the whole setting, whether it's a group of friends or an office party. You can only make the story work with some context that connects it to the others.

Your story context could be a scenario related to what someone among you had said during the party or earlier that day. It could be about a dinner you attended in the past. Ensure you are talking about some point everyone can relate to, and your story will be interesting. If you can achieve this, you have built a connection with anyone who listened to your story. Later, when you encounter any of your prior listeners, they will easily remember you and give you space to talk with them some more. Overall, storytelling helps you connect quickly.

- *Send the Right Energy*

Emotional energy is a powerful tool. Use it to build rapport and become a great communicator. Let your emotions come through when you're talking. This is how you bring other people into your world through your words. Emotional energy works like a magnet. Professional speakers use emotion in their speeches to draw their audience in and keep them in their world the entire time they speak. It's not only what they say; it's how they say it. Your emotional energy makes it easier to connect with others. You don't have to go overboard but put some emotional energy out there, and your listeners will react.

Non-verbal cues also communicate for you when you speak. Confidence, or the lack of confidence, shows outwardly. Speak confidently, or as confidently as you can. I find it hard to fake confidence. I have a way that works for me to avoid this problem. I ask for the other person's opinions. That way, the focus is off me and on the person or whole group. Asking for an opinion is a great conversation starter. People generally love to share their views. Saying, "I'm not sure. What do you think?" is an opportunity for you to be more open with others. They will be more willing to share their thoughts with you in the future.

- *Be Interested AND Be Interesting*

Again, humans generally like to talk about themselves. And for you to maintain or build a connection, you must allow space for the other person to talk. Remember that talking is the currency of connection. The conversation shouldn't be one-sided. Ideally, the flow moves in a way that both parties are involved. You show interest in what the other says by listening, maintaining eye contact, and possibly some slight head nodding. Then, you get to be interesting in return. The other person listens and displays the same physical cues as you did.

But what if they don't? You're upholding your end by being interested. The other person isn't allowing you to be interesting in return! You should feel free to disengage from the conversation at any point. You're not committed to being a sounding board for the evening. There are other people available who would welcome your thoughts and be receptive to listening to you.

- *Fun Conversation Starters*

Conversation starters are questions and statements that lead into a conversation. Whether you are talking to a stranger or a close friend, conversation starters help you begin or initiate your interaction. You can use them when talking with someone online or in person.

Conversations need to begin somewhere. A great way is to say something light and funny. The funnier you are, the higher your chances of getting a response from another person or people. Fun brings people together, giving them a reason to smile or laugh. If you can develop this skill, especially with someone you don't know, you will likely get them to continue talking with you.

Start by knowing the topic you want to talk about, then bring up a funny question or statement based on that. If you can get the other person's attention with this funny part, you will have their attention throughout your exchange. For example, suppose the topic of conversation is relationships. In that case, you could make a fun statement about how you had to chase after your partner before they finally agreed to go out with you. Alternatively, ask a funny question about any topic and, from there, continue your conversation.

Here are some fun and easy conversation starters:

1. What's the most ridiculous fact you know?
2. What is the best type of cheese?
3. What is the best kind of bread?
4. What is your favorite ice cream flavor?
5. What is the best purchase you've made?
6. What is the worst purchase you've made?
7. What is your biggest cooking disaster?
8. What is the most exciting thing you have watched this week?
9. What is the most interesting thing you have read this week?
10. What scene in a movie always makes you laugh every time you watch it?

- ***Deeper Conversations***

This kind of conversation goes beyond having everyday conversations with strangers, colleagues, friends, and family. Deeper conversations are more personal. The topics could be along the lines of life and death, religious or philosophical beliefs, or any other very private subject. People generally feel highly emotional about these subjects. Deep conversations are most often between people who have known each other for some time. There is likely the understanding among the participants that the entire discussion will be held in confidence. Deep conversations build long-lasting connections. People who have shared their most private feelings feel uniquely bonded.

If you're going to have a deeper conversation with someone you don't know well, there are still ways to go about it. The logic here is to start with a simple, easy conversation before introducing a deeper or more personal conversation. For instance, it might be your responsibility at your job to meet with subordinate employees to evaluate their performance. As part of this discussion, you need to understand their life goals. To begin the discussion, start talking about your career. Talk about the growth pattern your career has had in the past years. From there, you can ask what part of their job the other person enjoys and what they find interesting about it. To move to a deeper conversation, talk about your own career plans and ask the other person about their future and biggest dreams. The aim of starting your conversation with simple talk is to let the other person feel valued and to let them know you. Make them feel comfortable conversing with you.

Here are some questions to ease into a deeper conversation:

1. What is your guilty pleasure?
2. When was the last time you laughed so hard that you cried?
3. Which TV or movie character reminds you of yourself and why?
4. What topic could you give a 30-minute presentation on without any preparation?
5. What do you wish someone had taught you a long time ago?
6. If you could trade lives with one other person, who would it be?
7. What is your most bizarre pet peeve?
8. What is the strangest situation that you've walked into?
9. What would you change about yourself?
10. What is the silliest fear you have?

Look for a way to take a conversation branch (discussed earlier) into an area of discussion that will go a little deeper.

The location of this type of conversation is essential. Remember, some people want to avoid talking about their personal life in crowded places. In situations like this, a quiet area where you feel comfortable disclosing personal information would be best. If a private space isn't available, don't go into a deep conversation. Please keep it on the lighter side.

TECHNOLOGY CAN BE A BIG HELP

Unlike in the past decades when we traveled miles before being in touch with our loved ones, technology has made communication easier. With just a few clicks on your mobile phone or computer, you can easily connect with your friends, old and new. You can reach anyone, even in different parts of the world. A phone call, text, or chat will connect you with those you want.

The COVID-19 pandemic opened our eyes to the beneficial impact of technology in several aspects of our lives. There were days when we were at home running our business or doing our job from the four corners of our living room, not the four corners of the world. While this period brought a lot of misfortunes in terms of things we lost, many individuals successfully ran online businesses. The pandemic helped us connect virtually to our clients and customers. Beyond the business realm, we discovered we could contact and connect with our loved ones through the same technology. Many social media applications like Facebook, Instagram, Twitter, Snapchat, and Zoom are commonly used to communicate with others. Past research done by psychologists found that many individuals use social media to connect with their loved ones regularly. Cell phones and text messaging are good ways to communicate with people. These three, phone calls, text messaging, and social media have become vital parts of our communication.

Your Telephone Is Calling

A phone call to a longtime friend is an excellent way to connect with them. Telephone calling doesn't have to be done daily to connect deeply with those you love. My sister and I have recently decided to check in on the phone at least once a month. Before that, we relied on meeting at family gatherings which became very infrequent during the pandemic. The essential thing for us is that we recognized the importance of connection, and we decided to keep it going. It's easier to feel a sense of connection with people we speak with more often. It may be hard to take that first step to connect with people you have barely communicated with for some time. But it can be done.

You might feel it isn't necessary to call others. They know you love them, right? Using the telephone might be a stressful thing for you to do. If you do it anyway, you show the other person how much you want to stay connected with them. Usually, the person you call appreciates it more than you think they do. I encourage you to call that friend you've been missing.

Most people are pleased when you reach out to them. But what if you tried to reach out and felt the other person didn't respond well to your call? Then it's perfectly all right to let that relationship remain in the past. There is no need to feel bad about not connecting with someone who may not have decided to reconnect with you. In time, the unresponsive person may realize the benefits of reconnecting and reach out to you!

Telephone calling is good when you can't visit. Still, there is phone etiquette to be observed! First, follow the same guidelines as you would if it was a physical conversation. Please don't make a phone call to someone when it might be mealtime. There may be better times than calling in the early morning or late at night. Have an idea of the time that will work best for the person you are about to call. It's always polite to ask the person immediately if this is a good time to talk. If not, ask them to call you back when they're free. When you eventually speak with this person, keep the call short. Try to tune in to when the call should end.

Texting or Messaging

Texting is also referred to as messaging. The two terms are interchangeable. As with phone calls, texting can help you connect with people who are distant from you. Texting is very easy to use. Text messages are primarily used for quick communication. Texting has guidelines too. When texting a friend, colleague, or family member, you should do it when they are most likely to respond. Many people use the DO NOT DISTURB feature on their phones. That means the recipient of the message is not notified of it. You can set up this function to keep your phone quiet for intervals during any 24-hour period. I use this feature beginning at 10 pm every night. At that point, I want some quiet time. If you text and don't get a response immediately, you can assume that the person is unaware of your message. They will see the message if they check at some later time. You'll have to wait for their response. Find the best time to send text messages and allow enough time for the recipient to respond. If there's an emergency, make a phone call. Texting might only work for you some of the time. Be flexible. Using messaging can help you connect to people, but it has limits. It may not always be the right choice, especially if you want a long, deep conversation with the other person.

All of the following situations could be the basis of a comic movie! Yet they are true:

- Be sure who you're sending that message to before hitting the SEND button. You want to know that the right person receives the message.
- Chances are that you might make typos or grammatical errors while entering your message. Check it before you send it.
- Auto-correct can throw off your whole message! Scroll through your words again to make sure they make sense.

- Text lovers use abbreviations. Not everyone understands and knows how to use these. Type your words fully, so the other person can easily understand your message.
- If you get a message full of abbreviations you don't understand, just enter them into a Google search, which should clear things up.
- When you receive a message, try as much as possible to reply as soon as you can. Or reply to the sender by telling them that you got the message and will respond when you're free.

The Social Media Options - Pros and Cons

Several social media apps can also help us build long-lasting relationships with anyone. Facebook, Instagram, Twitter, Snapchat, Zoom, and many more are available. Suppose we wish to connect and maintain relationships with several people from different parts of the world. In that case, social media apps are the best bet. There has been a lot of debate on social media's benefits and detrimental effects. Yet, the advantages social media have offered us outweigh the disadvantages. Most of the problems associated with it can be avoided if we're careful. Here are some pros and cons of a few apps.

Facebook

Facebook remains the largest and one of the most widely used social media platforms, with over three billion users. Like every social media app, Facebook can easily be downloaded and installed on a mobile phone or laptop. People of all ages use Facebook, from children to adults, male and female. Anyone can easily connect with a Facebook account, which is easy to do by signing up with a username and a password. It's convenient to search for friends or make new friends from anywhere in the world. There are also interesting Facebook groups available to join. There are many Facebook communities where it's possible to learn about business, marketing, relationships, food, parenting, and nearly any topic imaginable. In any of the groups, we might find someone we genuinely want to be friends with and then connect with them on a more personal level.

One significant risk of Facebook usage is that scams are possible. Be sure to keep personal details private on Facebook. Giving out private info could lead to a mountain of trouble, including financial problems.

Instagram

With more than two billion users, there are always many people with whom we can connect. Beyond the pictures and fun things that allow us to communicate with friends, we can promote a business on this platform. Instagram uses the contact list on our phones to connect us with friends. Or Instagram can suggest new people with whom to connect.

Instagram is owned by Meta and has the same community guidelines as Facebook. The FCC (Federal Communications Commission) regulates Meta and all of its subsidiaries. Instagram still faces severe criticism because it has led many young people to develop low self-esteem and become seriously depressed, leading some to the point of suicide. Cyberbullying on this platform has increased suicidal thoughts by 14.5 percent and suicide attempts by 8.7 percent. Children and young people under 25 who are victims of cyberbullying are more than twice as likely to self-harm and enact suicidal behavior. Overall, teen suicide rates have increased the most within the past decade.

Twitter

Twitter is an excellent platform for connecting with anyone around the globe. Even though it has a short posting limit of 280 characters, it's particularly good at connecting people with the same interests. These include technology, gaming, education, sports, politics, science, and many others. Like many other platforms, it's easy to sign up and use and can be used by everyone.

Here we can find people with whom to discuss any compelling topic.

Twitter also has that cyberbullying issue! Arguments and misunderstandings are common among users. Most of these can be avoided by being careful with words and responses when discussing issues with others.

Snapchat

Anyone above the age of 13 can use this app. It is generally used to keep in touch with friends and share updates. It also allows us to send pictures and videos. The sign-up process is easy. A significant advantage of using Snapchat is that it doesn't store photos or videos for a long time, so while having fun, privacy is more or less guaranteed.

However, just like other social media platforms, many of the pictures and videos shared by some could lead to problems like jealousy, envy, and depression.

Zoom

The Zoom app became popular and widely used during the pandemic. It became indispensable when we were at home, but we still needed to move on with our lives. Jobs and education moved to Zoom. This platform is a great video conferencing tool. Although there are similar apps, Zoom offers users some unique features. It supports audio calls, video calls, and messaging to communicate among meeting attendees. Beyond its use for business and education, it can also connect with friends and family. It's free for a 40-minute audio-visual call with a friend or group of friends. To use Zoom for longer than 40 minutes, create an account and become a host. Hosts can set up meetings and record them for later use.

The greatest challenge with the app is Zoom bombing. This refers to unwanted, disruptive intrusion by internet trolls and hackers into video meetings. To prevent this, the host must set up a password for the meeting to keep it private.

Other Apps

There are very many more apps available. Linkedin is popular for business connections. Reddit is a comprehensive platform where people connect to share hobbies and interests. People use whatever suits them best. Remember that any internet activity has the potential for cyber problems.

The Social Media Take-Over

The most significant liability to social media and the online world is that some people spend most of their lives there. Social media has become part of the 21st-century lifestyle. The future is likely to see it become further ingrained into our daily lives. It isn't as harmful as it is beneficial. How we use and integrate these social apps and platforms into our lives determines whether it helps or hurts us.

I'm guilty of depending on the internet. When I was totally isolated from my former world, I turned to electronic media for everything. I went shopping on Amazon. I exercised with YouTube videos. I ordered groceries, so I only needed to park in the designated spot, and a lovely young person ran out to put the bags in my car. I also subscribed to a meal prep service that sent boxes of ingredients for me to put my meals together. I ordered restaurant meal delivery. Church was online. Facebook and TV became my daily companions. I met with my two best friends on Zoom when that worked for us. I tried family gatherings on Zoom too. I wasn't consumed with the apps that keep many people glued to their screens, but I depended on the electronic world.

I have another confession! I got most of the research for this book on the internet! It's easy to type in some keywords on Google and be flooded with information. There was so much information that I had to limit my topics here.

Current culture has accepted reliance on the internet and apps that help us out daily.

However, some people go beyond the limits of my dependency. They may have an actual addiction to social media. It can consume a significant part of their waking hours. It sometimes even intrudes on their sleep because they take their phone or tablet to bed. They don't put their phone down during family meals. They read or watch screens while walking, often leading to accidents with light posts and other permanent fixtures! Employers have a problem preventing employees from paying attention to their phones instead of working. These people are helpless to resist electronic notification sounds.

Social media addicts experience a feeling of living most of their lives through their screens. The terms that describe their behavior sound like part of a mindless cult. Streams of information from "influencers" populate their "feed." They "follow" people that they want to emulate. They compare themselves to impossible standards. The comparison between their real-life experience and their online influencers causes depression and a sense of hopelessness to achieve the lifestyles their idols seem to be living. They describe their online lives as a performance.

There's nothing wrong with a bit of fantasy. Addicted people fail to recognize that spending most of their life in a fantasy world interferes with real life. Since I didn't have that type of dependency, I asked those who have experienced it how they broke that kind of connection. How did I ask them? Online at the Reddit site, of course! Here are some of their responses:

- My tip is to get off social media. Or at least limit the social media accounts/apps that make you feel like you have to keep up with the influencers. I've been off all social media except Reddit for over a year. Best decision I've ever made.
- I deleted all my accounts (except LinkedIn because of some freelance work) cold turkey (even my old Reddit account). One day last year, I made just this current Reddit account. I wanted to be much more intentional about what media I consume and to break free of the constant pressure to "perform" my life.
- I've found news podcasts from a handful of trusted sources to be my best way to get prominent news so I would still be informed. Now I don't feel like I'm missing out or feel that pressure to perform all the time.

- I currently use social media (Facebook for Facebook Memories) and Instagram. I really only use it for messenger & memes to my friends. Now I also do things like Macrame, arm knitting, reading, and training my dog.
- I mean, the obvious response here is to get off social media, but I get that it's hard to do ... It's like dropping out of life. So change your social media. Pare down to one main one, fill your feed with accounts that align with your new life. Make your feed a mix instead of it being all just your high-living friends. Then a little at a time, drop the people whose posts don't feel relevant to you anymore or just make you feel bad.

Online Gaming

The online gaming world can also become an all-consuming addiction if players aren't careful. This seems to be a much more severe problem. The World Health Organization (WHO) has now classified gaming disorder as a mental health condition. Gaming disorder is similar to other addictions, such as gambling addiction or substance abuse. This disorder is characterized by the inability to control an obsession with video gaming. As a result, the need to continue the behavior increases over time. The main treatment option for video game addiction is talk therapy. Specific types of psychotherapy that may benefit someone with video game addiction include:

- Cognitive-behavioral therapy (CBT): This is a structured, goal-oriented therapy. A therapist or psychologist helps the affected person look closely at their thoughts and emotions. The purpose is for them to understand how their thoughts affect their actions. They unlearn negative and obsessive thoughts and behaviors through CBT for video game addiction and learn to adopt healthier thinking patterns and habits.
- Group therapy: This is a type of psychotherapy in which a group of people meets to describe and discuss their problems together under the supervision of a therapist or psychologist. Group therapy is a valuable source of motivation and moral support for people with this problem, especially if they've lost contact with friends or peers due to their addiction.
- Family or marriage counseling: This therapy can help educate loved ones about gaming addictions and create a more stable home environment.

I'd also like to add four short tips to avoid social media taking control of your life. These are simple but effective:

1. Turn off your phone notifications. This one is simple, but some people can find it hard to do.
2. Take a break from it every day. Allow for a given amount of time NOT to use it.
3. Don't use it immediately when you get up or before bed.
4. Remember these two facts: The purpose of social media is human connection. The purpose of online games is light entertainment.

FINAL CAUTIONS

There is very little regulation on most platforms except whatever the app provides. The US government remains unwilling to provide stringent safeguards. This opens doors for disinformation of all kinds to be spread. Please make a habit of checking for facts before you believe everything posted. There are several fact-checking apps on the internet, but using those is like asking the fox to guard the henhouse. There isn't an absolute way to verify the truth. Mostly I place my trust in major news outlets. For essential healthcare decisions, I trust my doctors.

Other countries own some social media apps. Personal information can be unintentionally extracted from us when we use social media. China owns Tiktok. At this point, we know data is being collected. We do not know its intended use. I personally don't use TikTok. I don't see any benefit in using this app. I prefer to be cautious about it. Everyone must choose what's suitable for their own lives.

YOU CAN TALK TO ANYONE

IN PERSON OR ON SOCIAL MEDIA

AN EASY WAY YOU CAN HELP SOMEONE ELSE

> "Communication is merely an exchange of information, but connection is an exchange of our humanity."
>
> — SEAN STEPHENSON

If you think back to the introduction of this book, when I told you my own story, you might remember that it was my friend who was the catalyst for the change I so desperately needed.

She saw how withdrawn and isolated I had become, and reached out with support and companionship. Her understanding and conversation empowered me to begin the process of reconnecting with others.

Just one person reaching out is incredibly powerful, and the wonderful thing is, it doesn't even have to be someone you know. Sometimes the kindness of a stranger is enough to help you see the world differently or give you the spark you need to drive yourself forwards.

This is what inspired me to write this book. That one person reaching out and letting you know it's okay is a powerful thing. You can do that for someone too (don't worry – you don't need to write anywhere near as much as I did!)

By leaving a review of this book on Amazon, you'll show other people who are struggling to connect with others where they can find the guidance that can help them – and you'll also make it clear to them that they're not alone.

Simply by letting other readers know how this book has helped you and what they can expect to find inside, you could be that helping hand that someone desperately needs – and it'll help you build your confidence in connecting with others too.

I know how isolating it can be when connection becomes more and more difficult, and I want to help other people find their way out of the darkness. Thank you for helping me to do that.

Scan the QR code below for a quick review!

4

ENGAGE IN LIVE SOCIAL CONNECTIONS

"We Can Bring Positive Energy Into Our Daily Lives by Smiling More, Talking to Strangers in Line and Replacing Handshakes With Hugs."

— BRANSON JENNER

Be brave and step into LIFE!

You can effectively create and maintain a healthy connection with anyone. Now that you recall conversation skills, why not go out and talk to someone? Talking is therapeutic; it might be all you need to reactivate your social life. This chapter will focus on the social benefits of talking to someone, what to talk about, and even how to talk to a stranger.

WING IT – JUST DO IT

The benefits of connecting with people are enormous. We've already discussed health benefits. Now we're moving on to psychological and social benefits. We may underestimate how much talking helps our psychological and social well-being. It's great to talk to someone, either a friend or a stranger. But is it easy and simple to come out of our shells? Absolutely not! Especially if we have been withdrawn from a social setting for a while. We will find that talking in person to others holds two specific benefits. These are confidence and self-assurance. The more we interact with others, the easier it becomes.

To consider the idea of talking to anyone outside your home and your family circle, I suggest a "social stretching" process first. This is very similar to stretching your muscles before you exercise. It involves moving gradually out of your comfort zone towards associating with others. It's okay to appreciate your private zone. Still, the goal is to move beyond your boundaries and relate and connect with several other people.

Research has shown that those who interact with others are more likely to live happy and healthy lives. People who live extremely private and lonely lives are more prone to social and emotional issues. Happy people are not free from these issues by any means, but they have a greater chance of living more enjoyable lives.

We're going to stretch ourselves socially to include more people. Remember that neighbor who walks by every day? Try and give her warm greetings tomorrow or try out a gentle smile aimed at a few people at the post office and observe the result. We want to gradually do something a little differently until we are socially reactivated. One of my favorite stretches is to confidently speak to the checkout person in the grocery store. I use full, clear sentences to see if I can get a response. A short conversation sometimes develops. This stretching exercise helped me take one more step towards rejuvenating my socializing power. I knew I was well on my way to social reactivation when I no longer automatically avoided eye contact with others.

SOCIAL BENEFITS OF TALKING TO SOMEONE

Everyone needs other people in their lives. We need to communicate our needs, wants, and goals or just let go of some internalized emotions. The ability to verbalize problems is crucial to a solution. A common saying is that a problem shared is half solved. Talking about an issue can help solve it. If you're facing no issues (yay!), a conversation could help someone else feel better and solve half their problem. Below are some sociological benefits of talking to anyone.

- *More insight into the situation*

Talking about a problem provides a clearer understanding of it and what it means to us. Almost everyone has the innate ability to solve day-to-day problems of life as they arise. Occasionally a problem or situation comes up that we're unable to solve. That's when we need to talk with a trusted friend or family member. Conversations provide insight into all the different aspects of the problem, along with some guidance and support. This is why it's important to share whatever we are going through with others. Conversations between friends allow for critical analysis. When we say the words out loud, we indirectly learn one or more things we haven't thought of before. I recall many "aha moments" when I talked to a friend and came upon an idea I'd never considered. We understand our world better by communicating with others.

- ***Make a better decision***

When we gain more insight into our problems, it becomes easier to come up with possible solutions. There are always multiple pathways to a solution. Our ability to make the best choice out of the available options will determine our chance of having a breakthrough. Input from a friend or loved one allows them to freely give us their suggestions and ideas. They could be supplying a concept we have yet to think of ourselves. This is also a circumstance I've experienced many times.

- ***Create support***

We often feel like the world is unfair when we experience one or two unfavorable situations. But some people have experienced or are experiencing precisely the thing we're going through. Knowing that others have overcome this problem gives us a sense that we're not alone. The situation is not unique. But how do we know this if we don't share our thoughts and feelings? By sharing the problem, we might discover that our friend has been in the same spot at some point. By speaking out and connecting, we'll get a firsthand account of how we can come to a breakthrough on this issue.

- *Release tension*

I've realized that when I share my problems, I feel relieved. This is because talking it out helps release some tension in my body. Talking with someone else helps me logically organize my problem. Before I start talking about an issue, my mind feels cluttered with thoughts. A conversation gradually allows me to see what is important and what is meaningless. Once the problem is organized into logical segments, it's much less stressful. The other person's point of view gives me new insight, relieving my stress. The more I talk the problem out, the more tension is eradicated.

- *Develop Those Communication Skills*

Communication begins with passing information from one person to another or an audience. Communication is only complete once the other person understands and decodes my information correctly. So, the more we learn to talk to people, the greater our chances of developing comprehensive communication skills. The give-and-take of conversation is the way the decoding process works. I say something, you add more ideas, and then I evaluate whether you have understood what I said. The process continues until we are both assured that the situation is clear. In problem-solving, clarity and understating are essential.

- ***Improve Problem-Solving Skills***

Talking to several people gives me a wider variety of ideas and knowledge about the world. When I constantly speak with friends, I get to know what they're facing, the dreams they're pursuing, and how they overcome their problems. This widens my ability to see beyond myself. For example, suppose my friend just got married. In that case, I'm sure some of our conversations are about how they're adjusting to a new lifestyle. In the future, if I eventually get married, there are tips I've already learned from my friend. In some way, I already know what to do if I face a similar situation.

Sometimes I feel like nobody wants to hear me vent. But the truth is there are people in my life who do want to listen and will gladly support me. Do yourself a favor; talk to someone today, and you'll be impressed with how much better you'll feel and how much help you can get.

- ***Proceed slowly***

Before the pandemic, leaving our homes and socializing with others was easier. I had what I considered a normal social life. During the pandemic, we had no choice but to stay at home. Many people have moved back to their former lives with no problem. I experienced a more complex return to my old ways of doing things. My stay at home during the pandemic definitely affected my socializing ability. I was overwhelmed, and sometimes I still am. To recover, I'm taking it bit by bit and working to return to my usual social self.

Here's another opportunity to involve your journal. Think of those things you used to do before to socialize with other people. Your old habits are no longer your current habits. For months your life has been different. To recover former habits, you have to introduce those things slowly. You need a plan. Make a list of all those activities, events, or situations that made you happy while being with others. Maybe you've been wearing a mask for some time and no longer find it necessary to do that. You may be out of the habit of using nonverbal facial cues. If you intentionally smiled at people before we were all wearing a mask where no one could see facial expressions, write that down. Recover that habit because nonverbal cues are a small but powerful aid in socializing. Go on to list other small things. Add as many little things as you can. After you've made your list choose one or two as your goal for this week. As you become more comfortable, add more to your goal.

Here are some more suggestions:

1. Phone a friend. Talk as long as you're both happy to do that.
2. When you meet a neighbor, chat for a few minutes.
3. If you are invited to a family gathering, go! Stay as long as you feel comfortable. Leave whenever you're ready.
4. Did you previously go to a gym? Go back at least once a week. Your body might demand more. Listen to it and go more often if possible.
5. Church? Go this coming Sunday. You can sit quietly for the service and leave asap if you need to. Or stay for the coffee hour if it feels right.
6. Go to a restaurant for a meal. Breakfast spots are generally not intimidating. You don't need to stay beyond the time it takes you to eat, and the waitperson may chat with you for a moment.
7. If you used to belong to a club, show up at the next meeting. Don't feel like offering an excuse for where you've been? Then don't talk about that. Deflect that topic. Talk about the weather or something else.

8. Write out some deflecting responses on another list.

WAYS TO BUILD MEANINGFUL SOCIAL CONNECTIONS

Now that we've taken a few steps toward reconnection, think about going further. Add on smaller steps to increase confidence and push forward into more solid connections. We might overlook the benefits of making small social connections. Still, the small things help boost success. Friends, family, and acquaintances surrounding us support us mentally, emotionally, psychologically, and morally. We know that the inability to connect with other people leads to loneliness and the cycle of isolation. Here are five additional ways to move forward and build stronger connections with others.

1. Improve current relationships

Our existing relationships need to be cared for and nurtured. These relationships need the investment of time and attention. Seeking out new people to connect with is a daunting challenge. Deepening an existing connection may be a better course of action. Remember those friends who have been there on our best and worst days. These high-value friendships need to be strengthened. People notice when the relationship is diminished. So be intentional about reconnecting. Reach out to them to improve or enhance existing relationships as much as possible. Instead of meeting in a public place, invite long-term friends to dinner at your house or ask the person to join you at a painting class or another activity you enjoy. The point is that the more you keep in touch with them and have deep conversations, the more you both feel connected.

2. Go to public places

If you're branching out solo, start easy. You may have just moved into a new area. You may have experienced a recent divorce and, with it, lost many friends. You may have lost a spouse and have been in mourning. When you're ready, simply going out can break the cycle, no matter your reason for avoiding public places. We often need to pay more attention to how many connections we can build by simply going to public places and interacting in a friendly way with other people. You don't need to stay long. Just go! Consider going to areas like a beach, park, museum, or library. Remember that you want to move just a little out of your comfort zone. See for yourself how those public areas feel, and do some people-watching. Say hello, or nod to others, and enjoy the moment. Doing this will make a big difference because you'll find it easier to visit any public place as time goes on. Gradually, be intentional about starting a conversation there. It doesn't necessarily have to be a long conversation. These steps are the basis for rebuilding social interaction. Soon you'll recognize "the regulars," and they will remember you. The goal is to initiate a social connection.

3. Find a group with a shared interest

An efficient way to build a meaningful connection with anyone is to join a group with interests similar to yours. It will be easier to have a flow of conversation and connect. When you're interacting within a group, your communication has shortcuts that everyone understands. The jargon and terms have a precise meaning to the group members. I used to belong to a group of IT professionals. We all dealt with one specific type of IBM computer. Those group presentations and the following conversations sounded entirely foreign to outsiders. Yet, we all knew precisely what the topic of conversation was about.

In any shared interest group, you can communicate freely about your common interest. Search the internet for your particular interest or hobby. For example, if you work as an accountant, join a group or an association of accountants. If you love to knit, find a knitting group. There is a group for any interest you may have.

People love to bond with others who share their passion. With time, you can move beyond the subject of the hobby and find other things you can talk about. If you find someone who seems open to you, explore other aspects of your lives where you might connect on a more personal level.

Making friends from the group is what we've been doing since early childhood. In elementary school, we remember pals and cliques who liked to be with each other. Attending school has, in one way or the other, helped us build relationships. At every stage of our lives, we have found a group of friends. Most adults are out of school, so meeting new groups of people has to be more intentional. People we meet from an association, volunteer group, recreational activities, etc., can provide us with new ready-made groups from which to make friends.

4. *Understand yourself*

While working on developing a connection with other people, take time to understand yourself. Most adults have a good idea of what makes them tick. You're well aware of your likes and dislikes. Before reaching out to a new individual, observe whether or not their personality will fit with yours. You already know that you're having a current problem reentering society. You're going to want to intentionally seek out another person who will help you with that, not hinder you. The other person might be too freewheeling for you to keep up. Or they may be in a more dire position on the social level than you are. It might take a few conversations to determine if a new person fits your idea of a semi-perfect connection.

There might be other reasons you don't click with a new group of people too. I remember when I thought joining a bicycling group was a good idea. It turned out that this whole group of people was training for 100-mile rides. No, thank you! I was able to bow out gracefully. They understood that I wasn't riding at their level.

Remember to celebrate your progress! What you're undertaking can be challenging. When problems arise, forgive yourself. Remember, the most important relationship in your life is with yourself. When you accept and appreciate yourself, you'll treat yourself with love and kindness. Stepping outside of yourself to connect with others will be easier in time. Appreciate, and be happy about every achievement you make. When you love and appreciate yourself first, you will find connecting with others easier.

5. *Reach out and be patient*

As we mentioned previously, plan what you want friendships to be like. Also, you can plan for how you want a friendship to develop. Are you single or part of a couple? Will your outings be double dates? Are you looking for another single person to accompany you to evening events like movies or dinner? Do you want companionship for hanging out at each other's homes? There are lots of opportunities and situations to choose from. Right now, I'd really love to have another single woman close by who would like spur-of-the-moment meetings for coffee or an evening glass of wine. I want casual conversation about any random subject.

When you have decided that a particular person is a good match for your personality, don't wait for them to reach out to you, be ready to do it first. As you continue to engage in meaningful conversation and activities with this person, you will be well on your way to establishing a great friendship.

When attempting connection, be patient. Good things take time. You may have to reach out more than once to show that you are serious about being friends. With time, you will build trust. If you really want to connect with someone, be proactive. Be conscious of the other person's reactions to you. If you're getting clear signals that this person isn't interested in the same sort of connection you want, then stop suggesting things to do together. You don't want to get into a situation that seems like stalking. You can stay casual friends and move on. Try again for the friendship you want with someone else.

WHAT WILL WE TALK ABOUT?

We've analyzed five ways to have a meaningful social connection with anyone. It's easy to begin talking on a topic with someone when you belong to the same group or association. You might feel uneasy connecting with someone you meet in a public place or with whom you are barely familiar. When situations like this occur, you will wonder what you should talk about, what the other person likes to hear, what your conversation should revolve around, etc.

Apart from the fact that you must first build rapport, you'll want to move your conversation to a more interesting level by focusing on one or more topics. Your conversation could revolve around neutral subjects like education, business, sports, parenting, food, hobbies, dreams, ambitions, family, or traveling. Your topic should be interesting, meaningful, and deep enough so that you can start building a connection.

With the use of a table, we have a handy list.

Topics	Things You Can Talk About
Family	You could ask the other person questions such as "Who is one person they admire in their immediate or extended family?" Let them tell you why they chose that person. Ask them what they think about family bonding and how a family can maintain a strong bond for years.
Entertainment	Ask about the song they most enjoy and why. Let the person tell you what the song means to them. Does the song hold a message for anyone besides themselves? You can also ask them about a movie they enjoyed that isn't popular or well-known by others. Then, let them tell you how the movie entertained them and what they gained and learned from the film. You could talk about your favorite celebrities. You could talk about which celebrity they like and what distinct personality traits a star has that seem interesting.
Friendship	Let the other person tell you what they love most about their friends. Ask them about friendships they have had for many years. Ask them what they do to have fun with their friends.
Business	Ask the other person what business they would love to venture into. Why do they feel that business has the best future in output or growth potential?
Parenting	What parenting style do they consider the best? Would they ever allow their kid to go to boarding school? What do they think about parents who don't live together with their kids?

The list of topics that can be discussed with other people is endless. That's one of the beautiful things about conversation. It can take off on one subject and flow to many others. During the discussion, take your time to notice the non-verbal cues the other person communicates. You will notice if they're interested in the topic; if not, you might want to change the subject of discussion.

GO AHEAD, TALK TO STRANGERS BUT BE SAFE

Often, we find it difficult to talk to strangers because of our false beliefs. When we were young, we were told not to talk to strangers or allow strangers to talk with us. We have since then held this belief that strangers are harmful and could be dangerous. But talking to strangers could be beneficial in several ways.

Strangers are people too! William Butler Yeats is credited with saying, "There are no strangers here; Only friends you haven't met yet." If we keep that idea as our guidepost, then any stranger we meet is a potential friend. That unknown person might be pleased to talk to us if we do it with good intentions. The moment a stranger understands that you only want to spend a brief interesting moment with them, they might become free and comfortable with us. You might discover that you have some things in common with this stranger, and they will be very willing to talk to you. The next time you go out, try it. Talk to a stranger and see what happens.

There is an actual sociological term for talking to strangers. It's called "minimal social interaction." University of Chicago psychologist, Nicholas Epley and his then-student Juliana Schroeder initiated a study where a group of people was instructed to speak with strangers on mass transit. They later reported a significantly more positive, enjoyable commute than the control group, who didn't talk to anyone. On average, the conversations lasted 14.2 minutes, and the talkers overwhelmingly liked the strangers they'd spoken with. They also found that people of all personality types had a good time. Another experiment, conducted in a waiting room, was designed similarly. In this one, some scientists were instructed to talk to strangers, and some were asked to remain quiet. The people who spoke—both the people who started the conversation and the people they talked with—reported having a significantly better experience than those who did not speak.

Keep Safety in Mind

Talking to strangers and connecting with them may be a great idea, but you must be sure you're safe. You will encounter many different types of people if you begin exploring talking to strangers. Remember to trust your gut instinct. Sometimes, you can guess what a stranger is like by merely observing them. If your instinct signals that you shouldn't approach a person, don't try talking to them. Below are some things to consider to ensure your safety while talking to strangers:

- **Only talk to strangers in safe places**

Avoid dark, deserted places. Only start a conversation with an unknown person in an area where there are plenty of other people. Talking to a stranger in a lonely environment could very well be dangerous. If you encounter a stranger trying to converse with you in an area where you don't feel safe, you don't have to respond to them. Leave as quickly as possible.

- **Don't get carried away**

If you meet someone who is a good communicator, chances are that you can start talking immediately. While this is happening, you should look at your environment to ensure your safety. Talking to a friendly stranger in a seemingly safe space where other people are moving around is okay. But the friendly talk might be a distraction to lure you into a less safe space. Be aware of what is happening. Don't be persuaded to move to a less secure area.

Consider your surroundings at all times. What if you're alone walking in an empty parking garage when someone who seems overly friendly approaches you? First, you need to know where you are in the space. Are you near an elevator or next to the stairs? Which floor are you on? Pay attention to what is happening around you. If you feel uneasy, take out your phone and call a friend to notify them of your location. A person with bad intentions will be less eager to harm you with your phone in your hand.

- **Do Not Disclose Too Much Information**

We might forget we're talking to a stranger when we meet someone who is free and open-minded. They might share their personal information with us, which is good because it helps us connect with the person faster, right? Maybe not! It could be risky if the stranger has a bad intention or when they are not actually who they say they are. In this situation, try as much as possible not to disclose your private information to strangers. There are neutral topics like education, food, music, etc. Just be sure you give your general view on those topics, not personal details about yourself. Avoid giving your full name, home address, bank details, and other personal information.

- **Don't Agree Unnecessarily**

You might be happy to meet a stranger who seemingly matches your personality. Your excitement about a lovely chance meeting could lead you to do whatever they suggest. Leave any conversation immediately if you feel the other person demands something you're not ready to supply or satisfy. If you're feeling pressured in any way, it's a sign that something is "off." Please exit as soon as possible.

- **Don't Welcome Strangers Into Your Personal Space or Home**

No matter how much you feel connected to a stranger, they are still strangers. Especially if this is your first time meeting them. We sometimes get excited when we meet new people with the same interest as us or with whom we would love to continue talking. Don't let the excitement get you to the point of inviting them home. Don't even describe your home to them. This is another point where your cell phone will serve you well. Call a friend, call a cab, call an Uber. If this person is going to become as special to you as you would like, they will have no problem letting you go. Make another plan for another public meeting. Take your time. Trust the process; as time passes, you will know if it's worth inviting them to your home.

How to Exit a Conversation if You Feel Uncomfortable

Either you are the one who initiated talking with a stranger, or the stranger did. Even if you're in a safe space, exit the conversation if you feel uncomfortable. Your safety matters even when you want to connect with people. While there are good strangers you can connect with, there are bad ones. It could feel awkward if you abruptly walk away or exit a conversation, but you must follow your feelings. There are several ways you can end a conversation.

- **Exit by saying thank you and goodbye.**

Let the other person finish the last statement they are giving, and tell them you understand perfectly what they have said. Tell them "Thank you" before wishing them goodbye. Then walk away.

- **Ask for directions to a nearby mall or restaurant.**

Tell them you need to get something important from a store or restaurant. Ask them which one is closest and how to get there. With this, they shouldn't have anything more to say, and you should go.

- **Tell the stranger you want to use a restroom.**

Tell the other person you need to use the restroom desperately. Immediately! Actually, go to the restroom. If it seems like a good idea, ask anyone there to walk out with you and stay with you for a short time until you feel safe. Most people will be glad to do that.

- **Excuse yourself to make an important phone call.**

Even at a party, this technique works well if you're unhappy with the conversation. You can easily quit a conversation by telling the other person that you need to quickly make a call you've forgotten about. Tell the friend you call what the situation is and ask them to stay on the phone until you're away from the speaker. You can walk away, talking on your phone. You can offer a little wave once you're in the clear.

If you want to continue talking with this person from a distance, you can ask for the stranger's phone number and then tell them you'll call later. This gives you a chance to decide whether or not you really want to talk more with this person.

- **Help the other person summarize what they said.**

What if this stranger or fellow party attendee is tiresome and long-winded? Another way to wrap up a conversation with anyone is to communicate to them that you understand all that has been said. Help summarize what they've discussed. Tell the other person you understand their point. If this is someone you don't want to offend, tell them you will get back to them soon. However, allow the person to finish their thoughts, so they don't feel awkward. Move out of talking range quickly!

YOU CAN TALK TO ANYONE

BUT STAY SAFE!

5

HOW TO FIND OR CREATE A CONVERSATIONAL GROUP

"All Problems Exist In The Absence Of A Good Conversation."

— THOMAS LEONARD

A conversational group may support you and others who have the same hesitation about making friends.

An informal conversational group can be a great help in connecting to others. You can share ideas, find solutions to problems, create opportunities, and develop meaningful close friendships in a group.

There are many kinds of groups. We already discussed hobby groups and business associations. Others promote community service, and some are involved in sports. You can find a wide variety of groups online or in person. Many groups may be close to you, within your local community. In the unlikely circumstance that there isn't a group for you, you can create one.

FIND OR CREATE SUPPORT

A conversational group is specifically designed to allow people to talk together with the goal of friendship. It doesn't have any other purpose. We will focus on conversational groups because conversation is our central theme. We'll explore information on where you can find a group to join and the benefits of joining or creating a group. Additionally, we'll discuss how to create your own group.

What is a Conversational group?

Conversational groups are sometimes referred to as mutual support groups. This group consists of individuals who come together to support one another. The members are usually people experiencing a common interest or issue. Sharing the same situation makes it easy for members to receive first-hand help from one another. The common interest doesn't have to be a problem. I've been in artist's groups and a group for mothers with young children, where we all chatted and watched our kids play for an hour. A conversational group differs from other support groups because everyone is focused on social connections instead of solving issues. Although, while becoming friends, some issues may be resolved along the way. People in a conversational group are comfortable sharing their thoughts and ideas. Group members find acceptance and, more importantly, practical advice.

Many people have associated some myths about mutual support groups, including conversational groups. We'll look at some of those and present the facts.

Myth - I don't have either type of group in my location.

Fact - Support groups exist in many communities, cities, nations, and across the globe. You may have to search for one. If you live in a big city with many people, it will be easier to find a support group. If you live in a small town with a homogenous population, chances are that you will still find some groups. You could join a group online or search 'Support groups near me' on Google to make your search easier. If you're looking for a conversational group and can't find one, we'll discuss how to create one later in this chapter.

Myth - These groups don't have solutions to issues.

Fact - Support groups do have the solution to most concerns. Humanity has not invented any new issues! Every human being has experienced similar problems in the past or is currently experiencing them. Individuals in the group may know ways to approach and overcome issues. However, any help or solution to a problem is generally offered in the form of group dialogue rather than one person presenting themselves as an expert. The person seeking a solution is free to take any advice offered or leave it. Please note that the group doesn't work magic; you must be ready to listen to the group to receive help. If you participate actively in the group, you may be surprised to find helpful suggestions to solve your issue. The knowledge and collective resources of the group are always more than an individual.

Myth - I will be required to share my problem.

Fact - Sharing your issues in the support group is not mandatory. It's a good idea to let the group know if you'd prefer not to speak, so everyone has a clear understanding. Some individuals join a group to ensure they are supported with their issues. It should be okay if you only want to observe. Even if you don't share your problem, you will get ideas on how to solve an issue from the discussions.

Myth - other members will criticize or judge me.

Fact - Support groups that are intentional about their structure and purpose will not allow criticism. Judgment and criticism are actively discouraged by members of the group. A healthy support group will have made its rules clear before anyone joins. One characteristic of a mutually led support group is that no leader or authority figure exists. Everyone is on the same level. Help or advice comes from the whole group, not a single individual. You may have to search a bit if this is the type of group you want.

Myth - My anxiety will increase when I join a support group.

Fact – Hearing other people's stories could trigger strong emotions if they correspond to your own issues. If that happens, consider the possibility that your problems are not unique to you. Others have experienced the issue before. While some members can easily handle stories from others, it could make some people tense and emotional. This might be because they identify so closely with that particular situation. Suppose you are an empathetic individual who will be troubled by hearing about other people's issues. You can continue looking for another group that will suit you better. There may be a similar group near you that won't be as stressful. It all depends on your ability to manage emotions. Not all groups will focus on highly emotional problems. Your focus should be on your reason for joining a group and what you hope to gain from it. A conversational group should be lighter in nature. It might be a better choice if you only want to talk and develop a healthy friendship within a group setting. Groups are unique and focus differently based on the members' needs and intentions.

YOUR OWN GROUP

MeetUp Groups

A helpful internet tool is called MeetUp. This tool is available for everyone to use. No matter where you live, you can access it. MeetUp is an online and/or in-person community that allows people with the same interest to find each other. Whether you like to party, travel, involve yourself with business, learn about tech, or anything else, you will find a group to join on MeetUp. This online platform connects interested people no matter where they may be. Once you find interested people online, you can meet them at a dinner event, go hiking or do some other activity. Many groups with different interests are on Meetup. Find one that interests you, and then join. If you can't find what you're looking for, you can create a Meetup for others to join.

It's important to note that it costs money to organize and run your own group (**between $9.99 and $ 14.99 per month**.) Using the MeetUp platform is easy. You must download the app, create an account, and search for a group. Suppose your interest is mainly in physical activity, like swimming or riding. You'll need to include your location in your search and join a community group. Meetup doesn't limit how many groups you can join, but if you want to meet people and make friends, stay active in any group you pick.

The MeetUp Group platform can also be used to create online events where people gather via their computers or phones. Meetup hosts some of the largest online groups. Some of the subjects of these groups are Entrepreneurship, Social Media Marketing, Online Education, and Professional Networking. These Meetups are free and not limited by location. Many people from around the world participate.

Pros and Cons of MEETUP GROUPS

The good things first! It's easy and fun.

- **Find a new interest to explore.**

I love learning new things!

- **Develop your social skills.**

There are specific groups on Communication, Self-improvement, Confidence and Self-esteem, Dating and Relationships, and Leadership. And many more.

- **Build your conversational ability.**

We will only know how far we can go with our communication skills by using them. When you join a group in MeetUp, you will have to talk with others, give your opinion on a topic, and listen. It's an excellent way to build your conversational ability.

- **Adapt to a new environment.**

If you've just moved to a new area where you barely know anyone, Meetup could be a great help. On your first Meetup, you might not necessarily make friends. Still, you will have the opportunity to relate and talk with a group of people. At your next meetings, you will become familiar with other people. You will be starting to build a community of friends. More importantly, if you let the group know that you just moved to town, you might get help navigating the city and having a lot of fun.

Cons

- **Live MeetUps aren't available in some places.**

MeetUp's popularity depends on people's ability to create, coordinate, and host events. MeetUp doesn't create the groups; people do. The group has to be created by someone before other people can join. If you live in a small town or village, you might not see a group within your community. You would have to be the one to create a group and invite people within your local community to join. Suppose you're near a city with Meetup events already organized. In that case, it is a good idea to travel there if it's convenient.

- **There could be a difference in age within groups.**

MeetUp is designed for adults who are out of high school. So anyone above the age of approximately 18 can use the platform. There aren't any other age restrictions or divisions unless a particular group sets its age restrictions. This can sometimes result in seeing individuals of several ages within a group. For example, you could see a group with a few members your age, but sometimes you won't see anyone your age within a group. If you want a friendship group where you can meet a friend your age, then search for age-range-specific groups. To communicate, you can also contact the members through their MeetUp profile in the app before the day of the event. If you're interested in meeting people of a specific age or any other feature, let them know you would love to see them at the event.

- **There could be cliques that form within the group.**

Forming a clique within the group is most times impossible to avoid. Some members could have known each other before joining the group. Apart from that, some members might have been in the group for a long time. They may have already formed a strong bond.

If you create a Meetup group

- **You can set the tone you want the group to have**.

When creating a Meetup group, the first thing to consider is the purpose you want the group to have. Be clear about what the group will focus on, what your event will look like, or the topics that will be discussed. Decide if most of your activities will be in person or online.

- **Plan the group basics.**

The next thing is to decide on the group's name and description. The group name should be simple, representing your group's purpose. The description should allow people to understand what your group is meant to be. Next, set the location, and be ready to manage the group.

- **Invite people of the same interest.**

The Meetup platform will help put your group in front of prospective members. You can also talk to people within your local community about it. You can invite people through your social media. Provide information on what the group is all about, what the group's mission is, and what people would gain from the group. Prospective members will want to know what to expect from the group.

Meetup groups are an excellent platform for everyone looking forward to improving on a skill or connecting through their hobby. It's a fun opportunity to build long-lasting friendships. Nothing is stopping you from exploring the platform.

YOUR OWN CONVERSATIONAL GROUP

You don't have to be a member of Meetup to create a group. Some of the steps to creating any group will be similar. You gather individuals with the same interest as yours and then form an online or physical group. Creating a group is generally straightforward, and anyone who has the desire can do it. You only need to be familiar with a few things to help guide and manage the group's structure. Your group does not have to be formal; it should just contain several people who want to come together to achieve a common goal or interest. Two goals might surface in our case, we want to make new friends or strengthen existing friendships. And we want to achieve a comfortable group of people who want to be together and support each other through conversation.

Setting Up and Managing Your Group

There are flexible ways to set up and manage a group. This will be an open, friendly, informal group. There are options as to how you would structure it.

- **Decide on the group's goal and purpose.**

Before setting up your group, be sure of what you want to achieve with the group. You will have to communicate these goals to prospective members. It's a good idea to write these down and make copies to give to prospective members. As you decide on what the group wants to achieve, this will guide you toward knowing what the group's participants will be like. For example, it could be a group of only men or women or a mixed group. The group could use a particular book and discuss one chapter at each meeting. Your group could have a definite purpose, like developing a skill or helping individuals overcome emotional issues.

- **Reach out to prospective members.**

Getting members for your group can be done in several ways. After deciding on the group goal and those that will fit perfectly into the group, it becomes easier to gather your group members. Think about where these people could be and then create awareness about the group. You could do this physically by going to places where they gather, like coffee shops or laundromats. If you have children, chances are that your kids have activities where you meet other parents. You can also utilize the power of social media. Tell people what the goal and mission of the group are. When you find others interested, be ready to suggest a time and place. You might even have slips of paper with your contact information and some details about the group. That way, people have a tangible reminder and a way to contact you. Be flexible about both time and place. If someone has a better idea, go for it!

- **Think about the facilitator.**

A facilitator in a group typically leads the meeting, ensures everyone is being carried along and reminds members of the group goal if necessary. Usually, in an informal conversational group, the facilitator's job is fluid. A conversational group is usually peer-led. This means that the group as a whole makes decisions. Someone will usually offer options to the group and help everyone decide on topics. Other decisions will need to be made from time to time, like changing the time or place based on varied schedules.

The group facilitator could be anyone, but since you are reaching out, it could be you. Although, if you're not comfortable with that, ask the group to decide on someone else if possible. The facilitator will probably be a natural leader who enjoys doing this. They could be any other person that the group chooses. Additionally, when everyone is familiar with how the group works, it will be easy for everyone to take a turn leading the meeting if they wish.

- **Decide on the organization of the group.**

A critical item in addition to time and place is deciding how long each meeting will last. Everyone should be respectful of other members' time. It's also a good idea to decide on a specific time frame for how long you will continue to meet. Will it be several weeks or months or during the kids' school year? That way, everyone has a better idea of how to commit their time. You don't have to be strict with these decisions. You might have to readjust them as the group evolves, but you must put them in place as you set up the group. On the date of the last meeting, have an Ending Party. I've been in groups before that had no specific end date. After a few months, it seemed like most people had lost interest and just stopped going. If this is happening, invite everyone back and have the Ending Party. The Ending Party is a final chance to connect and wraps everything up nicely. No one is left wondering what became of the group. Chances are that members have formed their own connections within the group, and hopefully, you have too. Those who want to continue their friendships are now well on their way to doing that.

Managing the group

One element of group dynamics is that, from time to time, problems will arise. The group facilitator needs to allow issues and concerns to be openly discussed. Other group members may have similar feelings. The facilitator is accountable to all group members and must ensure that member concerns are discussed and resolved as quickly as possible. Some measure of management is necessary, even in a peer-led group, to keep the group intact and avoid conflict and misunderstanding. At the first meeting, everyone should have a say regarding the "rules." Have some suggestions ready. Beyond time and dates, some group decisions should be made about conflict resolution and how it should be handled. All the decisions should be written down and printed so copies can be available at the next meeting. If more members are expected to join later, they must be made aware of the rules. It should also contain a definition of what peer-led means. For instance, **A peer-led conversational group depends on the group's consensus to determine topics of conversation and how the group will function.**

Any of the following topics can be included in detail. Don't get too bogged down. You can have any of these guidelines or not.

- **Confidentiality**

Everyone needs to agree that the details of the group discussions will only be repeated within the group. It's helpful to remind each other about the group's confidentiality often. A good trigger for a reminder is whenever anyone begins to share personal information. Confidentiality is a form of respect. No one's story should be discussed outside of the group.

- **Share ideas**

As you start meeting, you will find some members are very vocal and some are quiet. If the group is seated in a circle, it's easy to have an opening time for checking in, where everyone can say a few words about themselves and how their time has been since the last meeting. As the discussion takes off, the quieter ones may need some encouragement or a question explicitly directed to them to bring their ideas forward. Don't be forceful. Some members can sit out some of the discussions.

With time they'll blend in and feel free to talk within the group.

- **Respect**

Everyone within the group should be treated equally. Emphasize respect for all members. One way of showing respect is to observe the beginning and ending times of the meeting. Some members may need to be made aware of this fact. It should be discussed upfront. Waiting for people to arrive or having some come in late can be a problem. Also, when speaking, it should be understood that no one else speaks over them or interrupts.

- **Accountability**

If a member feels something is wrong within the group, they should be able to voice their concern.

- **Attentiveness**

Attentiveness is vital in every conversation. It's easy to have a side discussion with the person sitting next to you in a group. Discussions between group members in a sidebar are disruptive and disrespectful. When other members notice a side conversation, there should be an agreed hand signal to call for attention. It could be anything from a wave to a shushing gesture. Whatever you decide on, make it lighthearted and easy, not shameful. We are all guilty of this from time to time. Everyone wants to be listened to, and everyone wants to enjoy themselves.

- **Disagree constructively**

There will be instances when group members disagree with each other. It's essential to address disagreements when they arise. If an opinion is detrimental to the group, everyone has the right to discuss it. But this must be done constructively. The facilitator is responsible for creating a supportive and understanding tone that conveys appreciation for each member's opinion, especially the member whose opinion differs from most of the group. This is where the group has to manage itself. Differences of opinion are manageable, but navigating the differences can be tedious. If an unfavorable point is raised, further discussion should analyze it. The group should understand that the matter has various conclusions, and everyone is entitled to their beliefs about the subject. As the group works towards resolving the disagreement, the tone must be kept constructive. The goal is to identify and evaluate the common ground between group members and consider possible resolution pathways. After looking for possible resolutions, the group may not reach a solution. It doesn't mean that the group hasn't done its job. The group validated each member's opinion. It created a positive and supportive space and acknowledged that each person has their own beliefs. If no consensus can be found, agree to disagree and move on. No one should feel awkward about disagreement. It's part of what makes us unique.

- **Group Privacy**

Consider a location where you won't be disturbed. Depending on what type of group you have and what your group goal is, your spot for meetings might differ. A casual coffee club will not need as much privacy as a group that discusses personal matters. If you need privacy and can't find a neutral location, consider someone's home. In nice weather, an outdoor area might work.

- **Additional activities**

Besides having conversations, group members may add variety by including different activities or projects. This is especially true for groups with friendship as a goal. Various activities, like a walk in a botanical garden, a guided tour through an art museum, a book reading, or even quilting, could be planned. Suppose the group wants to help out in the community. They could plan outreach events or go as a group to volunteer at a charity such as a food bank. In a conversational group, the main point is to help the group bond and develop friendships. Activities for a conversational group have two purposes--deepening the group bond and developing friendships. There really aren't any limits on the types of activities that can be organized as long as the goals are supported, and the group members agree.

Meeting topics

The purpose of a conversational group is to have a meaningful conversation, but they don't have to be boring. Listed below are some questions that could spark lively discussions and help group members share their perspectives on life. You can use the questions as they are to generate discussion, or you can modify the questions to suit your group. If the group's purpose is to build friendships, it may want to discuss something other than Bitcoin Investment. However, the group may be interested in discussing their favorite podcast and what made Bitcoin enjoyable. The group may decide to take turns bringing questions to the group. Any question can spark conversation as long as it engages everyone in the group.

- Have you ever thought about how one member affects the whole group? How do you feel about this?

- Have you ever thought of being more appreciative for your entire life? What do you especially appreciate about your life?
- What if there was no such thing as a problem? What if we were only free-living human beings who don't experience any tough times? How would our world be if that were so?
- What would you do if a member is in crisis? Are you willing to help if you are the closest person to them?
- Would you want to do things with other group members apart from group meetings and activities? What fun things would you like to do?
- Ever thought of helping people who are in dire need? If you had unlimited resources? How would you help others? How would you go about doing that?
- Have you ever thought about the best things in your life, the best day, a place you've been to, your best friend, or something else? What are your all-time BESTS?
- Are you willing to put in the effort to participate in this group? What are the things you can do to make this a great group?

- Ever thought of being the funniest person on earth? If you were to achieve that, would you live differently?
- What are your innate problem-solving abilities? What could have been the hindrances to your ability to solve a serious situation you were facing?

Members can be on the lookout for more thought-provoking topics to discuss.

There are tangible benefits that can be derived from being a group member. A group could be all you need to rebuild your conversation skills or start a long-lasting friendship. If you have looked for a group to join and cannot find one that interests you, you can create your own group. If you do, you can fulfill your purpose while helping others achieve theirs.

YOU CAN TALK TO ANYONE
IN A GROUP

6

LEAVE ISOLATION BEHIND WITH GREAT FRIENDSHIPS

"Life Is Better With Friends."

— UNKNOWN

Develop the friendships you've been missing.

In our previous chapters, we've discussed many beneficial subjects that encourage us to break out of isolation. All of it leads us to our relationship with friends. Let's look at the different types of friendships and how the skills from the previous chapters can be used to make relationships with friends more meaningful.

Friendship means different things to different people. Ideal aspects of a friend would be someone who loves, cares about us, and appreciates us. Friends are willing to share many things with us, make sacrifices for us, and listen to us. They help us when we need them. Friends are ready to stand by and share our happy and sad moments. Unfortunately, sometimes these ideals fall short. We might see someone on one of the internet apps claiming they have more than a hundred friends. But that person may be without anyone who fits the ideal description of a friend. Close friendships are built with intention. We need to be particular about building solid, long-lasting friendships.

As we move through our journey in life, we meet different people. Some of these we choose as our friends. We hold on to some friends for a long time; some are short-term friendships. Unlike children, who tend to make friends easily, making friends as adults is more complex. But it's not impossible either.

BUILD LASTING CONNECTIONS

What does it take to make a friend?

How to start making friends with other people? There are some things to keep in mind, but it doesn't require significant effort.

- **Be willing to know others and yourself.**

Knowing your kind of person is essential. You are aware of a natural attraction to some people but not others. Some people want friends like themselves, and others want to be close to their personality opposites. Preferences differ. It comes down to knowing who you are and the type of friends you want. You may like friends who share the same career interest. Others want friends who hold the same values and beliefs. Your preferences provide a basis for understanding another person. If specific attributes are essential to you, then be sure to define this before approaching someone and beginning to build a relationship. Journal alert! Spend some time writing out a description of what you want your friends to be like.

- **Use those conversational skills.**

Naturally, you will need to talk with other people before you can build a friendship with them. Through conversation, you create a connection and then form a relationship. A conversation will determine if the other person will be a candidate to be your friend. Remember, conversation is social currency. It's valuable.

- **Explore as many places, groups, or communities as possible.**

You have to leave your comfort zone to explore. You can find people who might interest you in many places, communities, and situations. Your potential long-term friends could be anywhere. You can find friends in neighboring communities, recreational centers, workplaces, social media platforms, etc. You will only know once you look.

- **Nobody's perfect.**

Be prepared to deal with other people's weaknesses. We know human beings aren't perfect. Don't expect perfection, but there are limits to what we should tolerate in friendship. Personal boundaries are our rules that tell other people what lines they should not cross when it comes to what they say and do with us. Boundaries can be set informally during conversations. You can bring up the subject by mentioning a prior incident that happened to you or someone you know. You can stress that you wouldn't accept that behavior and ask your potential friend how they feel about the subject.

- **Don't apologize for setting reasonable boundaries.**

Boundaries aren't meant to limit other people. Boundaries are to protect yourself from unacceptable behavior. One of the reasons people might compromise their boundaries is because they feel guilty when they want their boundaries to be honored. It would be best to learn to ask for what you want without letting guilt get in the way. You deserve to be respected, and you are the one in control! Boundaries work both ways. During a conversation, your friend may have expressed their own boundaries. Once you both understand the limits, it becomes easier for you to form a healthy friendship. Friends learn to appreciate each other for who they are, their weaknesses, and their strengths.

- **What makes us attractive to other people?**

Respectability, responsibility, and openness are the primary attributes that attract others. Many psychologists have described more characteristics that are attractive to others, but they mostly all fall under these three categories. Let all of the best aspects of your personality shine! Add to that a sense of humor, and you are irresistible. Everybody likes to be with someone respectable, responsible, open, and funny! Let yourself be seen. To make friends with other people, communicate that you possess those three main attributes (plus humor). Then let your actions speak for your greatness. Above all, relax and be yourself. Be caring and considerate of other people. Make an effort, but don't be pushy. Be your genuine self. All of this communicates to other people that you don't just want to be friends but that you will make a good friend.

THE IMPORTANCE OF FRIENDSHIP IN ADULTHOOD

It's essential to have friends in adulthood. Friends help us through difficult moments and share happy times. Friends may be more critical than our spouses, kids, and parents. As we have discussed, having a solid network of supportive friends and family enhances mental, physical, and emotional health. Recent studies show that while the family is very important, strong friendships have an even more significant effect on our well-being than family. One reason for this is we choose our friends! Not everyone has family they are friendly with and can open up to. When we consciously choose to connect with certain people, we feel a greater sense of belonging. "The buzzword at the moment is a 'logical' family versus the 'biological' family. The 'logical' family is the family you would choose," says Sian Khuman, a psychologist and practice specialist in NSW, Australia.

- **Friendship helps cope with stress.**

In life, everyone experiences unpleasant moments at some point. Nobody has a perfectly structured life.

Stuff is going to happen. We'll all go through low times that make us question our existence. Stress could result from losing a loved one, job loss, inadequate finances, poor health, or any number of other issues. When we experience situations like this, finding someone to help us in the spur of the moment could be difficult or impossible. But if we have built a solid relationship with friends, they will support us until we're fully back in control. Just knowing that one or more friends are there for us helps us handle the stress. Helpful friends prove to you that you're not alone. Friends will let us vent all our frustrations, which releases a LOT of stress! The Harvard Medical School published a paper stating, "It [friendship] helps relieve harmful stress levels, which can adversely affect coronary arteries, gut function, insulin regulation, and the immune system. [And] Caring behaviors trigger the release of stress-reducing hormones."

- **Friendship helps Increase self-confidence.**

Knowing that someone cares and appreciates us is a blessing that can help us boost our self-confidence. A true friend can empower, encourage and support us. Friends give a much-needed outside perspective. Opinions from friends promote better decision-making. Friends can increase self-confidence by cheering on our successes and supporting our efforts.

- **Friends influence behavior.**

Unwanted or unfavorable behavior is common among young people. But even as adults, we still exhibit some undesirable behaviors. It could be unhealthy eating habits, inadequate exercise, or shyness. A good friend is an ally who will help us modify unwanted behavior without making us feel bad.

Remember to be a friend. If you have a friend you think needs help, let them know you're there for them. Even if you think there's not much you can do, listening and being supportive can help no matter what the problem behavior is. Remind your friend that they deserve the best in life.

- **Friends help us live happily.**

Friends will cheer us up when we're going through sad moments. They're there to listen to all of our favorable and unfavorable feelings. They're there to hang out with us and intentionally make us happy. A friend wants our happiness, and they'll go to great lengths to brighten our day. We all know of times when our friends have done some small thing that has had a significant impact on our outlook. These small things influence our lives.

- **Friends can help us achieve more.**

Sometimes, we get fed up! Ever experienced a time when you felt sick and tired of everything? Friends help us get through those times and help us achieve more than we thought we could. Having someone to share our experiences, ideas, and opinions will lift us out of depressing stretches. Friends can provide us with the motivation we need; they can encourage us to keep going. Friends add meaning to life.

HOW TO MAKE FRIENDS AS AN ADULT

Be willing to extend your circle. As we grow through different stages of development, from childhood through adolescence to adulthood, we have friends in various communities, groups, and locations. Think of where you were as a child. Do you still have friends from way back then? I'm lucky to still have a few friends from childhood with whom I'm in contact. Now think back to where you were as an adolescent. Remember those friends? That's usually a time of wild exploration for most people. Do you unconsciously smile when you remember these friends? Are there vivid memories of all the things you got into with those friends? All of these people and places are the fabric of our past. Where are you now? Is your location still the same, or has life brought you to an entirely different place? Who are the people that you consider friends now? Do you have as many friends now as you did when you were younger? If you're married, you may also have friends you've made with other couples. As we change our circumstances in life, whether location or stage of life, we extend our circle of friends to include those within our range of contact.

Avoid being so locked into past friends that you can't include new ones. It's possible to keep up with the great friends you've made in your earlier years, but be open to new people you will meet. Right now, please give a bit of thought or journal writing about how you are open to making new friends. Think about how you demonstrate openness. For instance: Joining a group or club, attending events, volunteering in your community, taking a class, etc. Remember to participate in conversations at these outings.

Be ready to make an effort. Making new friends as an adult can be challenging. Adults have to make friends on purpose. You know your personality's weak spots. Are there certain types of people you know you should steer clear of? Friends influence each other's personal preferences and lifestyles. This influence might be relatively trivial, but it could have a more significant impact. For instance, it can affect whether you choose to spend your money or save for a rainy day. It can also affect how you spend your time, like choosing to do charitable work versus spending more time chilling out with a glass of wine. Friends can influence each other's lifestyles, such as their eating habits and how they prioritize exercise. If you know that you need to stay away from people who will influence you to do things you'd rather not, then pay extra attention to those attributes of potential friends before making a solid friendship. On the other hand, if you see people who demonstrate all the things you want to cultivate in your life, you should definitely become friends with them.

Try new things. If your approach isn't working, change your course. Break your regular pattern. Try something different, anything different. Never been to a sporting event? Never paddled a kayak? Never joined a community theater? And when you find a new event, tell the person next to you what you're up to. Be open about your desire to connect with new people. Ask one person there what they think of this venue as an ideal place to find new friends. That's sure to kick off a conversation. You may be pleasantly surprised at the response you get.

If you feel resistant to going out, do it gradually. Try one new thing. Take one step at a time. Join a volunteer program. Go for a regular walk in the park. Attend the next party you're invited to.

Try out the friends-of-friends approach. This is an excellent way to meet new people. If you have a friend who has a friend that you like, you could start connecting with them through your friend. Many people have built connections and groups of friends this way. It's a reliable approach, probably as old as the caveman! And it will most likely go on forever.

A slight variation on the friends-of-friends approach is this. If you find yourself in a new community where you barely know anyone, your best bet could be recommendations from the friends you've made in past years. They might have a friend who lives near where you are now. Ask them for an introduction to people they know.

Your local community is an excellent source of likely candidates. If you are open to making friends in your neighborhood, you should find one or more people you can connect with. It could be someone right on your street or next door. If you're new to the neighborhood, someone may make a welcoming visit to your house or apartment. Don't let this opportunity slip by. Be sure to ask them to return and bring some people with them, even if you're knee-deep in packing paper and boxes. Ignore that and plan a coffee or cocktail hour at your place soon. Or ask them to take you to their hang-out spot one night soon. In most cases, people are always ready to go out at night, especially on weekends, to have fun and relax.

Your colleague at work might turn out to be a great friend. Pay more attention to opportunities to connect with people at work. While many people do this, others avoid it. You don't have to be friends with everyone at work, but you can build friendships with a few colleagues. Generally, employees understand a lot about the people they work with, like their personality, character, interests, values, and beliefs. And when you know this, you can easily decide who you want to be friends with. Then, invite the person you choose to a party or date, hang out with them, and talk to them about non-work issues. The average employee spends 81,396 hours — the equivalent of just over nine years — at work. You don't even need to go out of your way to meet this group of people! If someone turns you down when you suggest an outing, move on to someone else. Don't take it personally. They may have had a lousy work friendship experience in the past. Don't worry about it. No pressure!

Communicate how you feel to a potential friend. An excellent way to make a friend is to communicate to the person that you value them. You don't need to go overboard about this, but you could tell them how much you enjoy talking or hanging out with them. If you can achieve this, it becomes easier for the other person to connect and like you. Research has shown that we generally like those who like us. Feel free to let them know how you think of them. You're communicating your gratitude for having them in your life. Use phrases like: You're the best... I appreciate your help... you're fun to have around... thank you for your support with...

CHALLENGES IN ADULT FRIENDSHIP

We're bound to face some challenges in our friendships. Like every other relationship, friendship challenges are unavoidable, but they're worth working through. The challenges adults face as friends are as unique as the friends involved. The ones below are by no means a complete list.

- **Time**

Unlike the childhood or the adolescent stage of life, adulthood comes with many responsibilities that take away our time. We spend a lot of time on our careers, personal life, family, health, etc. This makes it difficult for adult friends to get together. The less time we spend together, the more our interaction suffers. Sometimes a friendship can fall apart entirely when the sense of connection is lost. Some friendships can go for quite a long time and then pick up where they left off. But some don't make it through a prolonged period of no communication. But, it could survive if you have a conversation or check up on them to find out what they're up to. That might be all it would take for you to maintain your friendship.

- **Expectations**

Expectations in friendship are a significant challenge. Friendship comes with explicitly defined and lightly inferred 'understandings.' One of them is that, as friends, we are meant to help each other through difficult times. This is a real test of friendship. We're sometimes surprised that some friends are only there to help us enjoy happy times. But it happens. Those who genuinely understand what friendship is all about will stand by you even in difficult times. It can take a lot of effort to help others through their hard times. Some friends aren't up to the challenge. Those who stay with us do it because they love, care, and appreciate us. Not meeting these expectations makes a friend feel they aren't appreciated, which could cause the relationship to fail.

- **Commitment**

Every relationship, including friendship, requires commitment. As friends, you need to communicate to one another that you are interested in the relationship and are willing to work hard so the friendship can continue. Unfortunately, lack of commitment has shattered many friendships. There is bound to be misunderstanding and conflict in any relationship we find ourselves in. But what keeps us going is commitment. When friends aren't committed to making their relationship work out, it becomes easier for the relationship to fall apart quickly.

- **Distance**

As we move through our life journey, it's common to move around. Location change could be necessary for job opportunities, marriage, acquiring more education, or other reasons. As we do this, friendships shift. While some friends still maintain their bond after changing their location, others find it challenging. Before you know it, you've already made another friend in the new place. Allowing distance to come in as a barrier in your friendship is quite common. I'm always impressed by one friend who goes to great lengths to maintain her friendships. She will drive throughout the state to attend birthdays and other life milestones for several friends. I think she is the exception. In my experience, maintaining a long-distance connection is the most difficult of all the challenges in friendship.

- **Status**

Adult friendships are sometimes based on financial or economic status. This, you wouldn't find in a childhood friendship. When we were children, it was easy to mingle with our peers irrespective of their appearance or what they owned. As adults, we often make friends with those we feel meet our status. But what happens when a friend experiences vast growth and development in their career while in the relationship? They might find other friends who meet their new status. This is a significant barrier to a lasting relationship.

- **Value**

A good friendship should be purposeful. Friendships on the more casual side are less supportive of the life goals of their friends. Those goals or achievements could be in any aspect of life. They could be moral, spiritual, emotional, mental, or economic. Friendships won't grow or maintain if one of the friends cannot derive some value from being friends. Friends shouldn't be dormant or passive in a relationship. Usually, when disinterest is communicated, the friendship ends quickly. This happens naturally. If you lack support, purpose, or interest in a friendship, there is no point in calling that person a friend. They're merely an acquaintance.

Responding to Conflicts in Friendship

Conflict in friendship is inevitable. Stuff comes up! Why are we shocked when this happens? It's only natural. Most issues can quickly be sorted out among friends if both parties clearly understand the situation and want to find a solution.

Trust allows us to feel safe with friends. We are safe to make plans and safe to share ourselves and our lives. Trust requires that we keep our promises and demonstrate dependability, respect, and honor. Being trustworthy means that others can rely on you to do the right thing. Your integrity and strength have been proven even to the extent that you would do something with significant personal risk, for instance, to your job or reputation, if needed.

Mistrust in friendship is disastrous and will cause the friendship to dissolve unless it's managed effectively. Mistrust occurs when friends lose confidence in one another or when either party finds it hard to believe in the other. Mistrust becomes a significant factor leading to conflict. There are a lot of reasons why distrust happens. If either of the friends notices this behavior in the other and fails to address it, assumptions will be created. In most cases, the assumptions aren't valid, but if they aren't dealt with, the situation could result in the loss of the friendship. The sooner friends talk it out, the better if they want their friendship to survive.

MAINTAINING FRIENDSHIPS

In addition to making friends, we must pay attention to keeping friends. Making good friends is challenging, but maintaining them will be easy once we understand how to do it. Research has shown that friends who are more deliberate about maintaining a friendship achieve more satisfaction than those who are careless about it. No matter the number of friends, the ability to maintain friendships determines if the relationship will be long-term, strong, and mutual.

Regular communication is essential. It comes down to staying in contact. The more we talk, the more we feel connected. Even if we're busy, we can create time for friends. Have a physical meeting possible. Visit or plan an outing if the distance isn't far. Plan where to meet, what to do when you meet, the fun places to visit, etc. Meet in person as often as possible. If it's not possible, use phone calls, video calls, or chats. There are ways to do this, including Zoom, WhatsApp, and Facebook. Even if friends live in different countries, staying connected with them is possible.

Celebrate their important days. Friends appreciate it when their birthdays, anniversary, or other joyful moments are acknowledged. Be available to celebrate with them if that's possible. If not, connect somehow around the time of the event. This strengthens your relationship and communicates that their lives are important. Failure to keep in touch this way will send the wrong message to the other person. The friendship will diminish if important days are ignored.

Help them out when needed. Our path won't always be smooth. And a friend in need, as they say, is a friend indeed. Learn to stay by a friend in difficult moments. Give them advice, encourage them, and help them see the brighter side of life. Assure them that things will change for the better, and stay connected with them in their hard times. I remember a time when I had to move out of my house. All my friends came together to help. That meant a great deal to me. Their help built a bond that I know will last. I'll never forget how they helped me, and I'll forever be grateful.

Buy them a gift or do them favors. Everybody loves gifts. No matter how small, it communicates to the other person your appreciation and that they are remembered. Or do some tiny favor, like picking up a grocery item on your way by the store if they need something. A little favor done willingly goes a long way to strengthening friendship.

Please share your opinion and seek advice from them as well. Be willing to share vital information with close friends. For instance, share ideas and knowledge to help them in their career, marriage, or education. You can also share household tips or recipes! Or trade babysitting time. The other person will rely on you for information and opinions that you bring to the table. Be willing to ask your friend for advice on a particular situation. The sharing of advice and knowledge is a two-way street.

Be understanding. Everyone can't be your best friend. Other people won't necessarily see life the way you do. So be willing to understand that some friends won't be as close as others. It's still advisable to understand the personality and perspective of these people too. Be ready to appreciate whatever gestures they might make toward friendship. Appreciate people for who they are and respect the limits of their ability to connect. In this case, you won't be disappointed when they do things you disagree with. You have already accepted them with their imperfections.

Do not share your friend's information with other people. I know you know this! Our friends trust us; they tell us things about themselves that they won't be willing to share with others. So, you must be able to keep everything your friend might have said to yourself. Your friend should be able to believe that their words are safe with you and they don't have to worry about a third party.

Friends are the BEST! Friends will help push you to achieve something you wouldn't expect you could ever do. They can help you live a less stressful life, help you live longer, and be happier. I have great friends who are doing wonderfully well. I am thankful for the friends and connections I've made over the past years. If you don't have a close friend, start to find and make one today. You can build a healthy friendship with someone you choose. Create the friendship you've always wanted.

YOU CAN TALK TO ANYONE
AND MAKE A FRIEND

CONCLUSION

Making a connection with another person might be hard work, but it's worth the effort. If you've followed me from the beginning of this book up to now, you have seen that it's possible. A healthy social connection with others can be created by following a step-by-step, intentional, and planned strategy.

We started by explaining what feeling isolated means and what causes it. The three significant factors, disconnection within ourselves, anxiety, and loneliness, all feed off each other in a vicious cycle, which produces isolation. Based on this analysis, we needed to check in with our mental health. We differentiated between normal mental health and mental disorders. At this point, and through the facts we gathered, we made it clear that a feeling of isolation doesn't relate to a mental disorder.

After establishing this fact, we began exploring other topics tailored toward helping us remember how to be connected with others. We looked at the benefits we would enjoy from being with others. We, intentionally or unintentionally, derive essential physical and mental health benefits when talking with and staying connected to other people.

We reviewed how to use conversation skills and get going with proven conversation techniques. We looked at practical tips that effective communicators and speakers use to keep their audience listening and some fun conversation starters. We later brought in how we can maximize the use of technology and social media platforms to connect with others. We discussed how to start talking to anyone, including how to handle talking to strangers.

We highlighted the importance of conversational groups and how they can help reestablish social connections. We talked about how to find or create a group and utilize the power of the MeetUp group.

In the book's last section, we discussed friendship and how necessary it is to build long-lasting and healthy relationships with people. We looked at how to start making friends, where to meet new friends, the challenges common to adult friendship, and how to conquer them.

Throughout the book, I have sprinkled some suggestions to use journaling as a focus for various subjects. Seeing my thoughts written out helps me analyze them. Keeping them all in a journal is my way of working on my issues. It's also a great way to go back and see my progress from one point to another. I know journaling isn't for everyone, but it helps me. Give it a try if you've never written out your thoughts before.

All of the information in this book mainly focuses on living a happy and self-fulfilling life by developing a strong social connection. The importance of building social connections is well documented by experts. Many of us have experienced first-hand social isolation and its harmful effects.

My purpose with this book is to show the way to regain our socializing power. Action, determination, and consistency are necessary to achieve that goal. Action first because that's the most significant hurdle to overcome. Talking – out loud to another human being - was the first action I took, and I encourage you to do the same. There is just no substitute! Determination will help you continue, while consistency will keep you going. I further encourage you to be constantly on the lookout for building and maintaining relationships with others.

I hope you're ready now if you still need to begin your journey out of isolation. Start bringing social connections back into your life. Talk to anyone today. Build or rebuild your lifelong relationships.

We can do this, and the best time to act is TODAY!

REACH OUT AND MAKE A DIFFERENCE!

Would you like an easy way to connect with someone else? You have a chance right now.

Simply by sharing your honest opinion of this book on Amazon, you'll show other people who are struggling to find connection where they can find the guidance they need.

Thank you so much for your support. As I said at the beginning of our journey together, we all deserve the happiness deep connections can bring us. Together, we can help others to find that fulfillment.

Scan the QR code for a quick review!

REFERENCES

5 Essential Questions For Leaders Seeking Lasting Friendships. . . (2018, December 19). Halftime. https://halftimeinstitute.org/2018/12/19/5-essential-questions-for-leaders-seeking-lasting-friendships/?gclid=Cj0KCQiAyMKbBhD1ARIsANs7rEFrqNC1Y83EKmaIzf9oBFF3aoKrwOWJZJV6VM93weoOqoIb2d6aEhcaArIwEALw_wcB

8 Ways to Make (And Keep) Friends as an Adult. (n.d.). https://www.betterup.com/blog/making-friends-as-an-adult

Abrams, Z. (2021, December 2). *How can we minimize Instagram's harmful effects?* https://www.apa.org/. https://www.apa.org/

Adobe Express. (n.d.). *The eight top social media sites you should prioritize in 2023*. https://www.adobe.com/express/learn/blog/top-social-media-sites

Aha-now, & SINGH, H. (n.d.). *Beware of These Friendship Problems*. Aha-now. Retrieved December 5, 2013, from https://Aha-now.com

Amsel, A. (2006). *Frustration Theory: An Analysis of Dispositional Learning and Memory (Problems in the Behavioural Sciences, Series Number 11)* (1st ed.). Cambridge University Press.

Christian, K. (2023, January 2). *99 Mindful Conversation Topics For Deeper Connections — The Good Trade*. The Good Trade. https://www.thegoodtrade.com/features/conversation-topics

Cohen, J. & PCMAG. (2020, July 16). *Twelve Tips for Staying Safe and Secure on Twitter*. www.pcmag.com. https://www.pcmag.com/how-to/12-tips-for-staying-safe-and-secure-on-twitter

Communication Skills - How To Improve Communication Skills - 7 Unique Tips! (n.d.). YouTube. https://www.youtube.com/watch?v=mPRUNGGORDo

Does Meetup.com Work For Making Friends? | www.succeedsocially.com. (n.d.). https://www.succeedsocially.com/doesmeetupwork

Foster, E. M., & Jones, D. E. (2005). The High Costs of Aggression: Public Expenditures Resulting From Conduct Disorder. *American Journal of Public Health*, *95*(10), 1767–1772. https://doi.org/10.2105/ajph.2004.061424

Goodman, P. (2022, December 21). *12 Disadvantages of Texting*. Turbo-Future. https://turbofuture.com/cell-phones/Disadvantages-of-Texting

Green, L. W., & Fielding, J. (2011). The U.S. Healthy People Initiative: Its Genesis and Its Sustainability. *Annual Review of Public Health*, *32*(1), 451–470. https://doi.org/10.1146/annurev-publhealth-031210-101148

Groome, D., & Eysenck, M. (2016). *An Introduction to Applied Cognitive Psychology*. Taylor & Francis.

Hogan, M. (2021, July 18). *15 eye-opening connection quotes · MoveMe quotes*. MoveMe Quotes. https://movemequotes.com/top-15-connection-quotes/

HOW TO KEEP A CONVERSATION GOING FOREVER. (n.d.). YouTube. https://www.youtube.com/watch?v=-TjTubAnHQE

How to start a group. (n.d.). Start a Meetup Group to Find People Nearby Who Share Your Interests. https://www.meetup.com/lp/how-to-group-start-v2-savings?utm_medium=SEM&utm_source=google&utm_campaign=mmrk_adwords_orgacq_us_save_branded&utm_term=group&utm_content=lp_grp_save&gclid=CjwKCAiA68ebBhB-EiwALVC-NiUJkqg0Foz9wiX3JcHwNUhSnE2gvsheOOxzhfiAWxMs33zKnEgu9hoCyCUQAvD_BwE

"I'm So Lonely": How To Build Meaningful Social Connections | BetterHelp. (2022, December 2). https://www.betterhelp.com/advice/loneliness/im-so-lonely-how-to-build-meaningful-social-connections/

Keohane, J. (2021, August 5). *Why We Should Talk to Strangers More*. The Atlantic. https://www.theatlantic.com/family/archive/2021/08/why-we-should-talk-strangers-more/619642/

Koen, L. (2022, February 1). *What Is Zoom and How Does it Work?* Softonic. https://zoom.en.softonic.com/articles/our-guide-to-using-zoom?utm_source=SEM&utm_medium=paid&utm_campaign=EN_US_DSA&gclid=Cj0KCQiAyMKbBhD1ARIsANs7rEFqQ3KmseUmJp5_pf_NW_Lcu2-nkMUtM8ymHTgvkT3ByngjiqR1mYYaAtNOEALw_wcB

Lin, J., MD, MCR, O'Connor, E., PhD, & Rossom, R., MD, MCR. (2013, November 3). Screening for cognitive impairment in older adults: a systematic review for the US Preventive Services Task Force. *Https://Www.Acpjournals.Org.* https://doi.org/10.7326/0003-4819-159-9-201311050-00730

Lind, A. (1997). Gender, development and urban social change: Women's community action in global cities. *World Development, 25*(8), 1205–1223. https://doi.org/10.1016/s0305-750x(97)00033-8

Lydia Ramsey, Savannah Morning News. (2020, November 4). *Twelve unwritten rules of texting you need to know.* Savannah Morning News. https://www.savannahnow.com/story/business/2020/11/04/twelve-unwritten-rules-of-texting-you-need-to-know/42993247/

Managing Negative Emotions: How to Deal with Anger, Anxiety, and irritation anywhere and anytime. (n.d.).

Nelson, J. (2022, January 27). *150+ Funny Conversation Starters Guaranteed to Get a Laugh [2022].* Thought Catalog. https://thoughtcatalog.com/january-nelson/2020/07/funny-conversation-starters/

Redirect Notice. (n.d.-b). https://www.google.com/amp/s/www.wikihow.life/Maintain-a-Friendship%3famp=1

R.N., A. S. (2022). *A Practical Guide to Overcoming Loneliness.* Independently published.

Rokach, A. (2019). *The Psychological Journey To and From Loneliness: Development, Causes, and Effects of Social and Emotional Isolation* (1st ed.). Academic Press.

Schwirzer, J. (2021, November 11). *Try Social Stretches for Anxiety.* Life & Health Network. https://lifeandhealth.org/mindfulness/try-social-stretches-for-anxiety/0821061.html?gclid=Cj0KCQiAyMKbBhD1ARIsANs7rEGel0CtF288G7PAxqfBEQTGrkagauOniaDGAppvs7Zho2lRaBGxhZYaAl5DEALw_wcB

Seligman, M. E. P. (n.d.). *Authentic Happiness: Using the New Positive Psychology to Realize Your Potential for Lasting Fulfillment.*

Seppälä, E. (2016). *The Happiness Track: How to Apply the Science of Happiness to Accelerate Your Success.* HarperOne.

Shrikant, A. (2022, September 12). *Your friends want you to call them more, new study finds—here's how to strengthen communication in your friendships.* CNBC. https://www.cnbc.com/2022/09/11/how-to-communicate-better-with-friends-advice-from-a-therapist.html

Simard, A. (2022a, October 6). *Friendship and Depression: Maintaining Friendships and How to Make New Friends.* HeadsUpGuys. https://headsupguys.org/maintaining-friendships-making-new-friends-depression/

Simard, A. (2022b, October 6). *Friendship and Depression: Maintaining Friendships and How to Make New Friends.* HeadsUpGuys. https://headsupguys.org/maintaining-friendships-making-new-friends-depression/

Smith, V. K. (2021, August 3). *How to Reenter Society Post-Vaccine, Even When You're Not Sure You're Ready.* Lifehacker. https://lifehacker.com/how-to-reenter-society-post-vaccine-even-when-youre-no-1847414032

Social Media and Mental Health - HelpGuide.org. (n.d.). HelpGuide.org. https://www.helpguide.org/articles/mental-health/social-media-and-mental-health.htm

Spanfeller, J., & Mejia, N. (2022, July 13). *78 Deep Conversation Starters To Help You Really, Truly Bond With Anyone.* Women's Health. https://www.womenshealthmag.com/sex-and-love/a37051626/deep-conversation-starters/?utm_source=google&utm_medium=cpc&utm_campaign=arb_ga_whm_md_pmx_us_urlx&gclid=Cj0KCQiAyMKbBhD1ARIsANs7rEEo5gsE1CuNGCP7Kxu8hHYvsj0YXp6ve475ym1tOgXyAXvkY6P4DGkaAqgFEALw_wcB

Starting a Support Group. (2023, January 24). The Well Project. https://www.thewellproject.org/hiv-information/starting-support-group#:~:text=Setting%20up%20a%20Support%20Group,-Partnering

Steiner, T. (2006). *Heart Circles: How Sitting in Circle Can Transform Your World.* Van Duuren Media.

Team, L. (2022, May 26). *14 Real Disadvantages and Dangers of Talking to Strangers*. Lifevif. https://www.lifevif.com/real-disadvantages-and-dangers-of-talking-to-strangers/

Telford, O. (2020). *Cognitive Behavioral Therapy: Simple Techniques to Instantly Be Happier, Find Inner Peace, and Improve Your Life*. Amazon.

The Great Age Reboot: Cracking the Longevity Code for a Younger Tomorrow. (n.d.).

Turner, J. (2022). *Being Present: Commanding Attention at Work (and at Home) by Managing Your Social Presence*. Amazon.

Waldmann, R. (2020). *STRESS HORMONES - Effects on the Body and Health: The Complete Practical Guide on Stress Hormones and Health and How to Recover from Chronic Stress, Fast and Easy (Complete List Added)*. Independently Published.

Wellness, U. (2022, March 28). *4 Reasons Friendship Is Important for Adults*. Urban Wellness. https://urbanwellnesscounseling.com/4-reasons-friendship-is-important-for-adults/

Yankovich, G. (2022, August 23). *How to Make Friends as an Adult, According to Experts*. SELF. https://www.google.com/amp/s/www.self.com/story/how-to-make-friends-as-adult/amp

Zoom Privacy Risks - The Video Chat App Could Be Sharing More Information Than You Think. (2021). Softonic. https://CNET.COM

Printed in the USA
CPSIA information can be obtained
at www.ICGtesting.com
LVHW091200211023
761202LV00006B/86